OLD TRA
POSTS

of the FOUR CORNERS

*A Guide to Early-Day Trading Posts
Established On or Around the Navajo, Hopi,
and Ute Mountain Ute Reservations*

by Richard C. Berkholz

Established 1921

WESTERN REFLECTIONS PUBLISHING COMPANY®

Lake City, CO

ISBN 978-1-932738-41-4

Library of Congress Control Number: 2006939933

Cover Art: "The Bullpen" by E. A. Burbank (Courtesy of NPS Museum, Hubbell Trading Post NHS)

Title Page: Drawing by Roland Brady (Courtesy of Evelyn Yazzie Jansen)

All photographs without credits are author's

First Edition

Printed in the United States of America

Western Reflections Publishing Company®
P.O. Box 1149, 951 N. Highway 149
Lake City, CO 81235
1-800-993-4490
westref@montrose.net
www.westernreflectionspub.com

To the early traders and their families who persevered in the loneliness and isolation of their remote locations.

CONTENTS

ACKNOWLEDGMENTS

The author gratefully acknowledges all the following traders, former traders, and others for their cooperation, friendliness, and patient assistance in providing the information that made this project possible: Jewel McGee (deceased); Charles Herring (deceased) and Grace Herring; Elijah Blair; Vernon Bloomfield (deceased); Kay and Russ Ashcroft; Don Walker, Allen Carson; Sylvan Jack (deceased); Clarence Jack; Harold Lampton; Clayton Bond; Walter Kennedy (deceased); Jack Cline; Maurice Tanner; Don Shillingburg; Earl and Birdie Ashcroft; Raymond Drolet; Bob Garlinghouse; Lamar Ashcroft; Bryon Pyle (deceased); George and Rena Savage; Mrs. Roscoe (Ruth) McGee; Russell Foutz (deceased); Bill, Jay, Lloyd, Jed, Decker, Phil, Keith, and R. B. Foutz, Jr.; Don Batchelor (deceased); Art Lee; Jeannie and Bruce McLaws; Robert Ismay; Raymond Bradshaw; Raymond Carson; Walter Scribner; John and Kathleen McCulloch; Don Reeves; Morris Butts; Joe Wright; Bob Lybrook; Mrs. Jane McDonald (deceased); Al Chapman; Ralph Brimhall; Danny Brimhall; Houston Walker (deceased); Mrs. Raymond (Marilyn) Blair; Mrs.Brad (Carolyn) Blair; Mrs. Troy (Edith) Kennedy; Mrs. Pat Tuttle; Mrs. Kathryn Bond; Dave Evans (deceased); Bill Palmer (deceased); Robert Bish; Clarence E. Wheeler; Walter "Bud" Gibson (deceased); Cliff McGee; Ferron McGee; Ron McGee; Robert Leighton (deceased); Andrea Ashcroft; Al Grieve; Floyd Burnham; Merle and Rosella Moore; Dan Christensen; Allen Christensen; Ray Hunt (deceased); Chuck Kinsey; Wally Anderson; Harold Randolph; Evan Lewis; Norman Ashcroft; Tara Travis (Historian, NPS); Don Biggs; Carl Morris; Ted Gonzales; Hank Blair; Paul Merrill; Dennis Dedman; Russell Griswald; Ralph Duran; James Nakai; D.J. Elkins; Bill Navarre; Rosalie Plummer; George Richards; Dale Underwood (BIA); Tom Taylor; Stan Martinez; Robert Cassidy; Lorenzo Fowler; Evelyn Yazzie Jensen; Al Townsend; Bruce Burnham; John Vidal (NM St. Parks); Mildred Heflin (deceased); Nina Heflin; Bill Crawley; Harold Bischoff (deceased); Ronnie Biard; Don Jensen (deceased); Sam Day III; Jay Springer; August Rudeau; Gordon Gorman; Bill Malone; Jack Powell; George Condeny; Colin Tanner; J. B."Buddy" Tanner; John

Yellowhorse; Betty Rogers; Larry Wilson (deceased); Jack Manning; Mrs. Mary May Bailey; Kay Borum; Ralph McGee; Jack Lee; Ferrell Secakuku; Tommy and Julie Canyon.

I especially want to thank Stewart Hatch, Lloyd Wheeler, Les Wilson, John Kennedy, John Arrington, and Fern Duckworth, who were full of useful information and provided many hours of enjoyable conversation. Plus a special word of thanks goes to Tomas Jaehn (Museum of New Mexico); Bart Wilsey (Farmington Museum); Ed Chamberlin (Museum Curator, NPS, Hubbell National Historic Site); and Edward Evans (Museum of Northern Arizona) for their photo assistance; to Duane Smith, author and history professor at Fort Lewis College, for his review of and comments on the manuscript plus helpful publishing suggestions; to Beth Green for her outstanding job in editing the manuscript; to Carol Lewin for her expert technical assistance and great work in preparing the manuscript for publishing; to Cristy Upshaw of Point to Point Graphics for all her time and effort in producing the maps. Finally, and most importantly, I thank my wife, Judy, for her review and editing, indispensable computer assistance, and especially for her company on my many trips to the reservations.

PREFACE

This is a book about Native American trading posts. Old trading posts. Trading posts that are still operating and ones that are long gone without a trace, except perhaps a crumbling wall or foundation. The book describes the present condition of each post, examines its history, and provides directions to even the hard-to-find posts. Indian trading posts are rapidly becoming a thing of the past or, as some would say, have become a thing of the past. Although many still occupy their original buildings, and some owners resist the complete modernization of their stores, few of today's so-called "trading posts" bear any similarity to what a real working trading post was once like. However, there still are a few in remote areas, far enough off the beaten path to function as old trading posts (with modern facilities). It is fascinating to visit them, talk to the traders or owners, and observe them dealing with local Native American clientele. The extraordinarily beautiful country in which many are located is further reward for the trip.

The trading posts have been rated from none to four stars based on their authenticity and historical interest. They have also been classified into the following five status categories:

Original — post is still located at the original site with minimal changes and its looks or functions remain similar to an old-time trading post.

Renovated — post has been remodeled and modernized, but it still retains some of the appearance and activities of a trading post.

Converted — post has been converted into a modern self-service convenience store, arts and crafts store, or otherwise no longer functions as a trading post.

Closed — post is currently not in operation, but could reopen.

Abandoned — post is permanently closed and there is usually nothing left but ruins.

The main focus of this book is the Navajo reservation. However, trading posts located on the Hopi and Ute Mountain Ute reservations are also included. An attempt has been made to include all trading posts, whether active or abandoned, in existence prior to 1950 and located on or immediately adjacent to these reservations. The reservations are located in that part of the Colorado Plateau known as the Four Corners, the only place in the United States where four states — Arizona, New Mexico, Colorado and Utah — come together at one common point. There is a monument, located just off US 160, forty miles southwest of Cortez, Colorado, marking the exact spot where it is possible to stand in four states at one time.

This book has been several years in the making, worked on as a spare-time project, albeit an enjoyable one touring the reservation lands and interviewing old-time Indian traders, their relatives, and acquaintances. Every effort has been made to make it as accurate as possible. However, changes may have occurred — owners change, posts close or modernize, and some may even have been eliminated. In an undertaking of this magnitude, it is also inevitable that errors or discrepancies will be found, and the author would welcome any questions, corrections, or comments. Much of the historic information was obtained through personal interviews and, like much oral history, is sometimes subject to question or interpretation. In addition, numerous books and publications were consulted and are listed in the bibliography. For those who might be interested in additional information, Frank McNitt's *The Indian Traders,* stands out for its complete coverage of the subject.

Millions of people travel through the high desert country of the American Southwest. Most know little about the old Indian trading posts or are completely unaware of their existence. You are invited to venture off the main highways and take a look at one of the few links to the Old West that we still have. I hope people will go and see the posts for themselves and experience the same vivid sense of the past that I experienced.

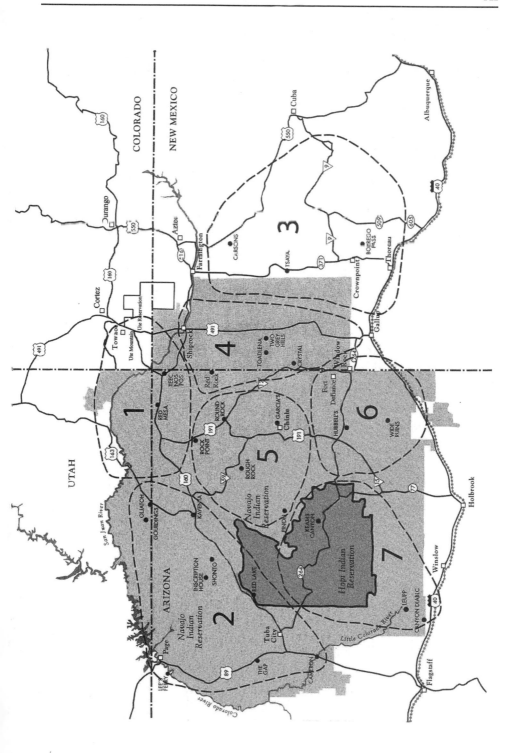

INTRODUCTION

INDIAN TRADERS AND TRADING POSTS.

History extols the bravery and enterprise of the pioneers, trappers, railroaders, miners, and cowboys, but little has been written about the romance and legends of the American Indian traders of the Southwest. Just when the first Indian trader began dealing with the Southwest Indians is uncertain. It is known that an 1849 treaty between the Navajo Tribe and the United States authorized trading houses in Navajo territory at the discretion of the government. Pack-train traders were present as early as the 1840s and '50s. These traders established no permanent posts but traveled around the reservation to common meeting places, not unlike the former trappers' rendezvous although on a much smaller scale. Other early traders sold goods out of covered wagons, moving from one Indian camp to another.

Trading posts, as we think of them today, first began to appear among the Navajos in 1868 after that tribe's return from confinement at Bosque Redondo, where a taste for Anglo-American goods was acquired. The posts were established at fixed locations where trade could be carried on out of a tent or building instead of wagons. The first posts were started in and around Fort Defiance, Arizona and spread out from there, particularly after the arrival of the Atlantic and Pacific railroad in 1882. The railroad allowed freight wagons to haul goods deep into the reservation from depots established along the rail route to the east and west of Gallup. By 1890, there were nineteen known trading posts established on the Navajo reservation, with thirty more at various locations just outside the boundary.

Many early trading posts were no more than flat-roofed sheds or tents using a board across two barrels for a counter. Later, if the post showed potential for success, it was improved into a more permanent structure. In establishing a post, the trader first determined where there was a sufficient population of Native American customers and then asked permission from their leader to build a post. He also needed a dependable water supply, and it was desirable to be close to the road leading to the wholesalers in town. Even after a good location was selected, many of the early posts were still temporary affairs with few improvements.

Since the traders did not own the land on which the post was built, there was always the possibility that permission to remain there would be withdrawn. Also, traders were required to be licensed, and this too could be cancelled at any time for political or other reasons.

Today, the situation remains somewhat the same. The trader owns the fixtures, inventory, and contents inside the building, but leases the building and land from the Navajo tribe. The current leasing arrangement began in 1953. Prior to that many traders believed they owned the buildings they had built. After the tribe and their representatives analyzed the legal aspects, however, it was decided that the tribe owned not only the land but also any improvements. The traders and tribe finally compromised with twenty-five year leases. In 1978, when the initial leases expired, the DNA (an abbreviation for a Navajo phrase meaning "attorney for the people") represented the tribe with a more aggressive and biased attitude against traders and trading posts. There were problems in getting many of the leases renewed. If the trader's lease was not renewed, or if he quit or moved, he could either sell out to another trader or give up the building. The Hubbell Trading Post is an exception because J. L. Hubbell owned his land and constructed buildings of a more permanent nature. Although the Hubbell Trading Post National Historical Site provides an excellent example of what an early-day trading post was like, it is not typical of the posts that existed during the time when it was established. Because of its size and the quality of its construction, it is considered the pinnacle of trading post construction.

Inside, nearly all early-day trading posts looked the same. There were high, rough wooden counters, sometimes four-foot high to act as a barrier between trader and customers. The counters were arranged on three sides around the front door forming an area where people could buy or trade their goods or just visit, tell stories, and smoke tobacco. This was often referred to as the "bull pen," and it often had a wood stove standing in the center. Usually chairs or benches were not provided since the trader did not want to encourage his customers' tendency to linger. The walls behind the counters were lined with shelves stocked with groceries, dry goods, tools, and utensils. Saddles, harnesses, bridles, blankets, kettles, oil lanterns, and other hardware hung from the ceiling. Quite often the floor behind the counters was slightly elevated to make the trader appear a bit taller, giving him a psychological advantage over his customers. Usually hidden behind the counter was at least one gun, always within easy reach. Up on the counter there might be a roll of wrapping paper on an ornate cast iron and wood holder, a cone of butchers twine, a coffee grinder, a plug chewing tobacco cutter, and a nailed down tin can with loose tobacco and papers to roll the traditional free "smokes." Occasionally nails were driven up through the bottom to encourage taking a pinch rather than a handful.

Typical interior of an early-day trading post. (Museum of New Mexico #12294)

Early trading posts were built out of whatever natural materials were available — stone, adobe bricks, or occasionally, logs. Usually in the same building and adjoining the store were the trader's living quarters, as well as a wareroom where merchandise was stored. Out back behind all trading posts there were large corrals maintained for sheep or other livestock brought in by Indians to sell or trade. Beyond the corrals were hay barns and one or more guest hogans for Navajo customers (who may have traveled twenty or thirty miles by horseback or wagon) to stay in while they completed their trading and selection of goods.

Indians traded wool, hides, blankets, rugs, jewelry, baskets, lambs, and other livestock for food, clothing, and tools. Some of the more popular items at the trading posts included coffee (almost always Arbuckles), flour, sugar, canned peaches and tomatoes, salt, bacon, potatoes, baking powder, lard, beef and mutton, shoes, hats, cookware, knives, saddles, bridles, needles and thread, calico, and velveteen. The Indians delighted in their trading ritual, spending all day at the post and negotiating each purchase carefully before buying it. Then they asked how much credit they had left before making their next purchase. A strict rule of behavior was observed — only one customer was waited on at a time.

When the Indians had nothing to trade they made their purchases on credit, pawning their old silver and turquoise jewelry, a fine hand-woven rug, a saddle, or some other item of value. Most posts had a special place, sometimes a vault, often a small room, where pawned items were kept. Governmant regulations required that pawn be held at least six months, after which it became "dead pawn" and could be sold. Most traders held items longer than the required time if it was a prized item and they knew the owner. Payday for the Navajo came twice a year — in the spring when they sheared their sheep and brought in wool and rugs, and in the fall when they brought in their lambs and bags of pinon nuts. In the early days little actual money was available and some traders made their own metal coinage, known as "seco." The traders would use it to pay for wool or a rug, and it was only redeemable at the store that issued it.

Trading posts were more than stores. They became the local meeting place, post office, and bank. The trader was a man of many hats and was often called upon to fill the role of doctor, legal advisor, arbiter of disputes, and even undertaker. Because of Navajo tradition against handling the dead, traders often would be called upon to wash and dress the deceased, build a pine coffin, and bury the person. The successful trader learned the language and would act as translator and spokesperson between the Navajo people and the U. S. Government or in any other matters concerning the outside world. All things considered, he was the best friend the Navajo had. There were a few exceptions where exploitation or unfairness occurred, but such traders usually did not last long.

Many changes have occurred to trading posts during the past fifty years. At one time there were over 300 trading posts operating on or around the Navajo Reservation alone. Today that number has dropped to fewer than sixty, with only a handful that even come close to what the original trading posts were like. The major changes began occurring shortly after World War II. Uranium mining and the oil boom, along with the social programs of the '60s, brought cash to the reservation and made the old practice of trading obsolete. With improved roads and the advent of the pickup truck, Native Americans became more mobile and traveled to bordering communities to do their shopping. Also, modern shopping malls have sprung up within the reservations. Many trading posts that remain have converted to self-service convenience stores selling groceries and gasoline but no longer trading goods for jewelry, rugs, wool, or livestock. Others, located along major highways, have become arts and crafts stores for tourists.

The method of operating has also changed. In 1970 there were more than sixty trading posts on the Navajo reservation that provided credit to their customers and accepted pawn. Today only a handful provide limited credit, and Navajos have to travel off the reservation to pawn their jewelry and valuables. One exception is at Tuba City. The pawn system existed until 1972 when Federal Trade Commission hearings on trading post practices resulted in new regulations so restrictive that, within five years, the practice ceased at reservation trading posts. The new BIA (Bureau of Indian Affairs) regulations on pawn resulting from the FTC hearings, new leasing regulations enacted by the Navajo tribe, more competition from new stores opening on the reservation, plus the increased mobility of customers, have all led to the closing of many trading posts. Once a post is closed, it is usually only a matter of months before vandals take everything that can be used and destroy the building. The remains are cleaned up, leaving hardly a trace of previous occupation.

Yet some of the earlier, long established posts survive, if not on the exact same spot or in the same building, then very near or in buildings that evolved from the original. They hang on in a transition between the old-style trading posts and the new self-service stores, filling a need that the more modern replacements cannot provide. Trading posts were, and still are, a place for the Native Americans to gather and visit. For many they are still the source of their food, fuel, and feed for livestock, as well as a source of income through the sale or trade of their arts and crafts, livestock, wool, and other items. As long as this need exists there will be trading posts, in one form or another.

THE NAVAJO.

By far the largest Indian reservation in the United States is Dine'Bekahi — "Navajoland." It consists of nineteen million acres and is located in northeastern Arizona, northwestern New Mexico, and the southeastern corner of Utah. It also abuts the Ute Mountain Ute Reservation in the southwestern corner of Colorado. Over these acres are scattered more than 220,000 Dine'— "The People"— the name they have given themselves. They make up the largest Native American tribe in the United States, occupying a reservation that is larger than the states of New Hampshire, Massachusetts, Connecticut, and Rhode Island combined.

The Navajo immigrated into the Southwest 500-600 years ago from northern Canada and are descended from Athabascan-speaking people. The earliest evidence of their presence in the Four Corners region came from the remains of a hut found in northwestern New Mexico dated around 1541. They were nomadic hunters who settled among the already-present Pueblo Indians, intermingling with them, learning agricultural techniques, and borrowing from their culture. After the Spanish arrived and introduced sheep, the Navajo settled into a life of farming and herding.

In the late 1700s raiding and warfare started between the Navajos and the Hopis, Utes, Zunis, and Pueblo groups; the Spanish; and then the Mexicans after their independence from Spain in 1821. The United States displaced Mexican control in 1846, but the raiding continued. To end the conflict, after a series of unsuccessful treaties, the U. S. Army in 1863-64 invaded the Navajo homeland. Under the command of Colonel Kit Carson a "scorched earth" campaign was conducted, killing people and livestock, destroying homes and crops, and taking much of the tribe captive. In what the Navajo call the "Long Walk," soldiers marched the survivors, some 7,000 people, nearly 300 miles to Bosque Redondo, a reserve in eastern New Mexico near Fort Sumner. They all went on foot, with only an occassional horse to carry their few crude possessions. Many perished during the walk, with more than 2,000 dying during their four year internment there.

Finally, on June 1, 1868, a treaty was signed allowing the Navajo to return to their own land with enough sheep to begin rebuilding their lives. That year the U. S. government officially established the 3.5 million acre Navajo Indian Reservation in parts of Arizona and New Mexico. When they returned to their new reservation, some stopped short of the boundary and settled on lands they had previously occupied. The reservation was enlarged in 1880 to include additional areas in New Mexico, but much of the area where the Navajos had resettled was not included. Later, in 1911, much of this land was designated as public domain and opened to homesteading. Today this area, known as the "checkerboard," is divided into units usually one mile square designating Indian, Federal Bureau of Land Management, state, and private lands, with much of it having been consolidated into larger units through purchase and land exchanges.

Photo courtesy of Fern Duckworth

The Navajos have subsequently acquired ownership of much of the area, but it is still not officially part of the reservation.

Three decades following their return from Bosque Redondo everything was going well and the Navajos were starting to show signs of prosperity when a major natural disaster struck. In December of 1898, the worst winter storm in the memory of pioneers struck northwestern New Mexico. Twenty-four inches of snow fell and the San Juan River completely froze over with ice twelve to fourteen inches thick. The river became an ice road between Shiprock and Farmington. Navajo flocks starved or froze to death, and thousands of sheep were lost.

However, some sheep and goats survived, forming the nucleus for future flocks which increased rapidly. By 1931, the number of sheep was estimated to be nearly a million with more than a third of a million goats. In this semi-arid country, it can take 20 acres of land to support one sheep, 120 for a single horse, 100 for each cow. Overgrazing coupled with years of drought caused severe erosion, and Commissioner of Indian

Affairs John Collier, at the urging of the Soil Conservation Service, introduced a stock-reduction program that eliminated nearly 25 percent of the sheep and almost 70 percent of the goats. The tribe had gone from conditions of abject poverty caused by the severe winter of 1898 to affluence and then back to poverty conditions. The severe winter of 1898 combined with the stock reduction program had a disastrous effect on the Navajo people which is still felt today.

The Navajo Reservation embodies some of the most awesome and spectacular scenery in the United States. Within its boundaries are found more than fifteen national monuments, tribal parks, and historical sites. Frequently visited attractions include Canyon de Chelly National Park, Monument Valley Tribal Park, the Little Colorado River, Rainbow Bridge National Monument (discovered by Byron Cummings in 1909), Chaco Culture National Historical Park, Hubbell Trading Post National Historical Site, Navajo National Monument, Window Rock, Four Corners Monument, and the Bisti Badlands.

It is a geographically diverse area with rugged mountains, high plateaus or mesas, deep canyons, deserts, fertile valleys, and spectacular rock formations. Elevations range from 3,000 to over 8,000 feet. Because of the relatively high elevation, extreme summer heat is uncommon, yet the sky can be cloudless for weeks. In winter there may be from a few inches of snow at lower elevations to several feet in the mountains. The warm sun, however, prevents any lengthy winter season. The mountains are green with pine, spruce, and fir. The plains and mesas have pinyon and juniper, native grasses, sagebrush, greasewood, and creosote bush. During the rainy season and spring snow melt, the arroyos and natural ponds are filled with water, and most of the desert produces enough grass to winter graze the flocks of sheep. There are many areas with enough moisture for families to grow corn, squash, beans, and melons.

There are few towns in the familiar sense. Navajos are not community-oriented, but rather live together in small clans or family groups scattered across the reservation. A small cluster of hogans, a trailer, and a house or two may be home for three or more generations of one family. However, in recent years this has changed somewhat on parts of the reservation with the advent of modern tribal housing projects. The hogan is the traditional home of the Navajo. It may be used as a dwelling or for ceremonial purposes. Its octagonal shape is believed to have originated in the 1880s, and it is constructed of whatever materials are available — logs, earth, stone, lumber, even concrete.The doorway always faces east, allowing the occupants to greet the new day with the warmth of the rising sun.

The current form of Navajo tribal government was established in 1923. Prior to that time it was governed by a clan system with a common language. Today, there is a Tribal Council consisting of an elected tribal president, a vice-president and eighty-eight council delegates representing 110 chapters (local units of government) from throughout the Navajo Nation. Chapter houses provide places where members can gather for social events or for formal meetings of the chapter and are a good source of information when visiting the reservation. Council delegates meet a minimum of four times a year as a full body in Window Rock, Arizona, the Navajo Nation capital. The capital is named for the large, red sandstone arch located in a park behind the tribal council chambers.

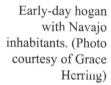

Early-day hogan with Navajo inhabitants. (Photo courtesy of Grace Herring)

Window Rock at Navajo Nation Headquarters, Window Rock, AZ.

THE HOPI.

The Hopi have long been inhabitants of the Southwest and are thought to be descendants of the Anasazi (now referred to as Ancestral Puebloan people) who inhabited Mesa Verde and other sites in the Four Corners area of the Colorado Plateau. By the twelfth century they began to settle at the present Hopi villages. The Hopi village of Old Oraibi is believed to be the oldest continuously inhabited town in the United States, established around 1150. The Spanish were the first Europeans to make contact with the Hopis around 1540. They came looking for gold and stayed on to make slaves out of many of the Hopi. The Hopis tolerated the Spanish until 1680 when they joined in the Pueblo Revolt and forcefully expelled them from their land. The Spanish returned twenty-one years later and resumed their domination. This led to a second revolt at Awatovi around 1700, pitting Hopis against Hopis. In 1821, the Mexicans gained control following their independence from Spain. The Hopis came under United States jurisdiction in 1846 following a treaty between the U.S. and Mexico after the Mexican War.

In contrast to the more nomadic Navajo, the Hopis were a stationary people and today live in centuries-old villages clustered on or around the First, Second, and Third Mesas in the southern half of their reservation. Villages include Hano, Sichomovi, and Walpi on First Mesa with Polacca at its base; Shungopavi, Shipaulovi, and Mishongnovi on Second Mesa; and Hotevilla, Old Oraibi, and Bacabi on Third Mesa with Kykotsmovi (also known as New Oraibi) close to the bottom of the mesa. Each village is independent, practicing its own style of government. All Hopi villages have gifted artisans, and distinctions can easily be made between the crafts produced by different villages. The First Mesa people are known for their Hopi polychrome pottery. The Second Mesa people specialize in Hopi silver overlay jewelry and coiled basketry. The Third Mesa people produce works of wicker and twill basketry.

The Hopi Reservation, surrounded on all sides by the vastly larger Navajo Reservation, was established in 1882 when Chester A. Arthur was president. It was originally 2.5 million acres in size. Many Navajos, however, already lived on lands that were made part of the Hopi Reservation. Because of the Navajo encroachment and the federal government's unsuccessful attempts to settle land disputes between the two tribes, the Hopi reservation was reduced to 630,000 acres in

1962. The remaining 1.8 million acres belonged to both tribes and became known as the Joint Use Area. This did not work out, and in 1974 the land was divided equally between the tribes. Dividing the JUA required relocating several thousand Navajos from ancestral homes that were in Hopi territory and moving about 150 Hopis from Navajo lands. Legislation was enacted in 1996 to help resolve this unfortunate situation. During the tenure of Hopi Tribal Chairman Ferrell Secakuku, the Accommodation Agreement was drafted and approved by both tribes, which established the final resettlement procedure. However, problems still exist with the actual implementation of the agreement in certain areas of the Hopi Reservation.

THE UTE MOUNTAIN UTES.

The Ute Indians are believed to be the oldest continuous residents of Colorado. It is not known exactly when they arrived from the north and west to inhabit the mountainous areas of Colorado, Utah, and New Mexico. They are not believed to be descendents of the Anasazi (Ancestral Puebloan people). In fact, it is possible that the arrival of the Utes was the reason the Anasazi moved into the cliff dwellings and eventually left the area.

Historically, the Utes roamed throughout this region in a hunter-gatherer society, moving with the seasons for the best hunting and harvesting. Eventually, they became concentrated into a loose confederation of seven bands. The bands were further broken up into small family groups for a large portion of the year. It was necessary to do this because food was scarce and it took a large area in the mountains to support a small number of people. This way of life changed when the Utes made contact with the Spanish in New Mexico in the 1630s and '40s. The introduction of the horse enabled the Utes to range over a much larger territory and hunt buffalo on the eastern slope of the Rockies. The horse became a prized possession of the Utes, and they would even trade children (usually captured from the Paiutes and Navajos) to the Spanish for horses. They also became more aggressive and warlike and began raiding other Indian tribes and non-Indian settlements for horses.

During the late 1870s and 1880s there was much controversy about the removal of the Ute Indians from Colorado. In 1880, the Southern Ute Reservation was established in southwest Colorado, but it wasn't until after 1895 that an agreement was reached on its implementation. The Weeminuche Band, which in the meantime had moved to Utah, was forced back to Colorado but refused to return to the old agency and established a camp at the western end of the Southern Ute Reservation. In 1897, a sub-agency was opened for the Weeminuche Band at Navajo Springs which was located about three miles south of present-day Towaoc. This separation was the final regrouping for the three bands of the Southern Ute Indians into the two existing tribes we have today. The Weeminuche Band became known as the Ute Mountain Utes with headquarters at Towaoc, Colorado and the Mouache and Capote Bands are known as the Southern Utes with headquarters at Ignacio, Colorado. The Navajo Springs agency was abandoned in 1915 and relocated to Towaoc. In addition, the Tabeguache, Grand, Yampa, and Uintah Bands now constitute the Northern Utes, located on the Uintah-Ouray Reservaton with headquarters at Fort Duchesne, Utah.

The current Ute Mountain Ute Reservation consists of more than 597,000 acres in Southwest Colorado and Northern New Mexico with a tribal enrollment of over 1,900. Today, the Ute Mountain Utes enjoy a modern lifestyle, while retaining many of their traditional customs.

VISITOR ETIQUETTE.

The Native Americans of these reservations welcome you to their homeland. However, certain rules and restrictions should be followed. All travel is restricted to designated public roads (federal, state, county, and Indian). Permission must first be obtained from tribal authorities to venture off these roads, and in some cases a tribal member or guide must accompany you. They are proud to have you photograph the beautiful scenery of their reservations, but please ask permission before taking pictures of people or their personal property. Some do not want their pictures taken, and others may request a small fee. When visiting Hopi villages, it is wise to first inquire at the Hopi Cultural Center or the Tribal Headquarters at Kykotsmovi about which villages are open and what restrictions may apply. Photography, sketching, or recording is never allowed in the villages. If visitors are allowed to witness a Hopi ceremony, they should be respectful and not ask questions. Knowledge of the various customs is helpful. Among the more traditional Navajos, direct eye contact is considered impolite. Likewise, touching can be a sign of disrespect. Usually only a handshake is considered polite and then a gentle touch of the hands is sufficient and preferred. Use of firearms and all alcohol and drugs are prohibited on the reservations. Archaeological, natural, and cultural resources (including the remains of old trading posts) are protected by federal laws and should be respected.

Chapter 1

Four Corners

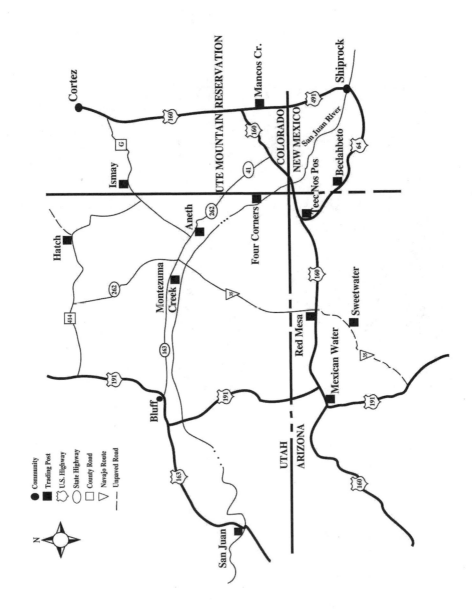

Ismay Trading Post★★★★
391 Co. Rd. G, Cortez, CO 81321, (970) 565-7752

Located on Co. Rd. G, 26 miles west of Cortez, CO.
Rd. G leaves US 160 about 2 miles south of Cortez.

Description: *Original.* This old post is definitely off the beaten track. It is still located at its original site and little or no changes have been made to either the exterior or interior since it was built. The building is constructed of adobe with a stucco overlay. The interior is sparse and functional, maintaining the original bullpen design. The post carries a limited inventory of groceries and sells gas and other items needed by the local Navajo and Ute population. There is also a small supply of rugs and other arts and crafts, but tourist business is not a priority.

History: John Ismay established the post in 1921. Ismay's sons, Robert and Eugene, took over the post in 1958, and Robert continues to operate it. The Ismay family gave the site for Yucca House National Monument to the national park system and also gave many artifacts to Mesa Verde National Park. This post is one of the few old-time, authentic stores still in operation and is worth a visit just to see that they still exist. It probably won't be around too many more years. The road travels through a green valley with beautiful reddish-pink rock formations. Occasional scattered old ranches make an interesting backroads trip. The recently established Canyons of the Ancients National Monument is located on this road and about a mile beyond the Monument is the last remaining one-room school house in the state.

Hatch Trading Post★★★★
P. O. Box 364, Blanding, UT 84511

> *Located on Co. Rd. 414, about 6.6 miles east of its*
> *intersect with UT 262; this junction is 15 miles north of*
> *Montezuma Creek, Utah.*

Description: *Original.* The building in which the trading post is housed is constructed of native stone painted light tan and is quite authentic looking. There are wood and cement block additions built onto the back and sides of the store. In addition to the post there are numerous other buildings and corrals out back. The interior decor is plain and functional in the fashion of many of the older posts, with a sparse inventory designed to meet the needs of the area Navajos. It carries a limited amount of Indian arts and crafts, but does not cater to the tourist trade. The grounds around the post are attractive and well-kept with numerous willows, large cottonwoods, elms, and other species, all of which were planted since 1960. The many trees growing about the post give it the appearance of an oasis in the desert.

History: It is believed that Roy Rutherford started the post in 1903. Rutherford sold it to Joseph Hatch in 1924. Two years later, Joseph's father, Joseph, Sr., helped build a new post a short distance away, this being the current trading post. Joseph, Jr.'s brother, Ira Hatch, took it over in 1927; and his son Sherman, the current owner, assumed ownership in 1949. After taking over the post, Ira acquired several sections of land around it, all of which have been disposed of except the 320 acres on which the post currently sits.

San Juan Trading Post★★
P. O. Box 276, Mexican Hat, UT 84531, (435) 683-2220

Located in Mexican Hat, Utah, on US 163 just
before crossing the bridge over the San Juan River.

Description: *Converted.* The trading post is housed in a two-story building with the lower level made of native red sandstone and a frame addition built on the upper level, which is used for a residence. It is the original building at this site and has an authentic appearance that blends in with the surrounding country. The interior has retained much of its early-day decor and has not been greatly modernized. The store, which no longer functions as a trading post, sells some groceries, but mostly deals in Indian arts  and crafts. There is also a restaurant adjacent to the store in a separate building, plus a large, two-story motel located to the rear, all of which are of frame construction with a stucco overlay. All the facilities are perched on a high bench directly above the San Juan River.

History: The early history of this post is unclear as to when or who started it. Frank Pyle bought it from Card Bowen around 1925, and it is possible Bowen was the first owner. Emery Goodridge had a trading post in the area in the early 1900s. Whether or not this was the same store is uncertain. Pyle sold his post to Art Spencer around 1928 or '29.

In 1933, Claude and June Powell became the owners and then sold it to Ray Hunt. Hunt had owned an earlier trading post reported to have been started in the 1870s and located close to Mexican Hat rock. He closed it and moved away in 1932 to operate other posts. He returned in 1939 and bought the post (then called Mexican Hat Trading Post) from Powell. He operated it for five years, leased it for three years to John Johnson, and then turned it over to his brother, Jim Hunt, in 1947. Hunt owned it until his death in 1973. Jim's wife sold it a year later. The restaurant and motel were added by Jim Hunt in 1955, and he renamed it San Juan Trading Post. Subsequent owners include Barney Walker, Jerry Baum, and the current owners, Mark and Julie Sword, who bought it in 1983. The present bridge, located just past the trading post, is a replacement of the original suspension bridge built in 1909, which was the only crossing of the San Juan River at the time.

Montezuma Creek Trading Post★★

Located on UT 162, 1.8 miles west of Montezuma Creek, Utah.

Description: *Abandoned.* The original post burned in 1978 and was rebuilt the following year. It burned again in 1988, with heavy damage to the interior. It has been vacant since the last fire and was recently torn down and the site cleaned up. Only a cement slab remains.

History: The name of the original trader and the date of establishment is uncertain, but it is believed to have been started by Billy Young around 1918. Other owners included Progressive Mercantile in 1927 followed by Roy Rutherford, who sold the post in 1948 to Wilford "Wiff" Wheeler. Wheeler's son Lloyd took it over from 1955 until 1963. He was followed by Lamar Ashcroft who sold it to Fern Matthews, the last owner, in 1976.

Lloyd Wheeler related an interesting story as told to him by his father about Poke and Posey, a couple of mixed Ute/Paiute renegades who inhabited the area around Montezuma Creek and Bluff, Utah. Posey was the meanest, was supposed to have killed several people in the area, and had everyone, both white and Indian, running for cover when he came around. Posey was eventually killed by a posse with a rifle shot from nearly a mile away. He crawled up into a rocky cliff to hide, where he was found dead by the posse.

Another story written by Frank Pyle tells about "The Uprising of Polk and Posey in 1915." Polk's son shot and killed a Mexican in a robbery on the Ute reservation somewhere in the vicinty of Cowboy Springs. He ran to the Ute camp and hid. When the Indian police went to the camp to find him, his people would not give him up. The same thing happened when the sheriff and deputized men went to get him. Shortly thereafter, Polk and his son, along with several other Utes, left for Bluff, Utah. The local sheriff and a U.S. Marshall from Salt Lake City tried to take the young Indian into custody, but without success. A posse of about thirty men from Cortez and Dolores, Colorado, was organized and sent to Bluff. They planned to surround the Native Americans and surprise them early in the morning, hoping to get them to surrender without any trouble. However, an old Indian woman came out of a tent, saw them, and began screaming. A running gun battle ensued the rest of the morning and one deputy and four or five Native Americans were killed. Later that morning, Posey and his band, who were camped about a mile or two away, heard the shooting and came

Polk, aka Billy Hatch, was a Ute who lived in the area around the old Navajo Springs agency south of Towaoc, CO, in the 1920s. (Photo courtesy of Stewart Hatch)

riding up behind the posse. They shot one man and cut five others off their horses and stole them. Things quieted down in the afternoon and by the next morning the Native Americans had slipped away. A few days later General Winfield Scott arrived in Bluff and persuaded Polk and his son to surrender. The boy was taken to Denver to stand trial. He was kept there for a few months and then released. About two years after he returned to his people, he died of tuberculosis.

Aneth Trading Post★★
P. O. Box 1, Aneth, UT 84510, (435) 651-3244

Located on UT 262, 18 miles northwest of its junction with US 160.

Description: *Converted.* The store became less of a traditional trading post shortly after 1965 and was converted to a convenience store and gas station when Thriftway Corp. took it over. The current store is a fairly

large, painted structure with twin peaks giving it the appearance of two buildings being joined together. This is the result of two enlargements which took place in 1958 and again about ten years later. The original post was well built of cut stone, portions of which are still in use as part of the current store.

History: Aneth, originally called Riverview, was established by Oen Edgar Noland in the late 1880s. Noland sold the post to Pete Guillet, who had managed the store for a year prior to buying it. Guillet then sold it to his half-brother Sterl Thomas, followed a short time later by sales to A. J. Ames and Jesse West. There has been a succession of owners at Aneth ever since, including Tom Dustin (1910), John Hunt (1918), Dick Simpson (1921), Bob Smith (1926), Ralph Tanner (1935), Ralph Tanner and Elijah Blair (1953), and Roscoe McGee and Elijah Blair (1955). It was operated by Roscoe McGee's son-in-law, Claude Petty, from 1965 to 1971 and by Roscoe's son Dwight McGee from 1971 until 1979, when Thriftway acquired it and subsequently transferred it to Red Mesa Express in 2001.

Trouble occurred at the store shortly after Noland started it. Noland's father-in-law, Stanley Mitchell, who was operating the store for Noland, became involved in a quarrel with a Navajo which unfortunately resulted in the Navajo's death. Mitchell fled to the Four Corners Trading Post, located about six miles upriver and took refuge there. The Navajos laid siege to it for a week. Noland was finally able to get word to Fort Lewis, and a small force of cavalry arrived and restored order.

Old Aneth Trading Post on San Juan River, about 1900. Second and third man from left are Butch Ames and Jesse West, respectively.

Mancos Creek Trading Post★★

Located on US 491, 23.5 miles south of Cortez, CO.

Description: *Abandoned.* The original post was located adjacent to the Mancos River on the old road from Shiprock to Cortez about two and a half miles west of its later location. A description of the original post given by Carr McGee's daughter, Fern Duckworth, states that it was a two-story building made of cut sandstone blocks with a corrugated tin roof, which housed the store, wareroom and living quarters. There was a large barn, made of rough lumber, across the road, plus a mud and log hogan for overnight visitors. The newer post, located on the highway, was constructed by Carr McGee and was built of adobe, made on the site, and lumber was hauled in from Mancos. It had a combination residence and store, hay barn, visitors hogan, and other out buildings.

Original Mancos Creek Trading Post on old road between Shiprock, NM, and Cortez, CO, 1935. (Photo courtesy of Fern Duckworth)

Last Mancos Creek Trading Post which was located on US 666 (currently US 491) south of Cortez, CO, about 1940. (Farmington Museum, #1996.3.7)

History: Frank Pyle established the original post in 1923. T. H. Akin was Pyle's partner and financed the store until Pyle took sole ownership in 1925. In 1926, a western movie, entitled *Scarlet West* and starring Clara Bow and Johnny Walker, was filmed in the area. Frank Pyle recruited the Native Americans, both Ute and Navajo, who took part in the movie. Shortly after, the post was completely destroyed by fire, and Pyle immediately rebuilt it. Dan Tice and Card Bowen became the next owners in 1928. They in turn sold to Dan Walker and John Claflen with Walker eventually taking it over. Elmer McGee, the next owner, turned it over to his cousin, Carr McGee, in 1936. Carr moved it to US 666 (currently US 491) in 1938 shortly before his death in a tragic car accident. The McGees had started to Kirtland, New Mexico, and when they crossed the state line the highway changed from pavement to loose gravel on the New Mexico side. Their car skidded out of control and turned over, killing Mr. McGee.

Carr was followed by a series of owners which included Roscoe McGee (1939), George Bloomfield and Raymond Blair (1944), Raymond Blair and LeRoy Bish (1954), Brad Blair (1961), Floyd Stock (1963), Pete Corey (1964), Norman Smith (1975), and finally Nancy Redfield (1982). The lease with the Ute Mountain tribe terminated in 1989, but Redfield actually closed the store three years earlier in 1986. After the post closed it sat vacant for ten years and gradually deteriorated from vandalism. The store was finally burned down by the Ute Mountain Ute tribe in the summer of 1996. The remaining buildings were torn down the following year, and the entire site has been cleaned up.

The site of the original post can be visited, but you must first obtain permission from the Ute Mountain Ute tribe at Towaoc, Colorado.

Four Corners Trading Post★★★
Ute Mountain Ute Tribe, Towaoc, CO 81334, (970) 565-3751

Located on the northeast side of the San Juan River about three miles north of the Four Corners Monument. For additional directions and permission to enter Ute land, contact the Ute Mountain Ute Tribe at Towaoc, Colorado.

Description: *Abandoned.* Initially the post consisted of a stout structure made of cottonwood logs which housed the store and living quarters.

Later, a large stone warehouse was built onto the west end of the original

Gun port at Four Corners Trading Post.

Remains of Four Corners Trading Post. Note man standing at far right corner.

post, with small gun ports built into the walls for defensive purposes. The trading post and living quarters may have been moved into this structure, which was L-shaped and over 120 feet long. The walls, which were nearly twelve feet high, are still standing and in good condition. This was an amazing structure considering its size and the amount of stone used in construction.

History: Oen Edgar Noland built the post, known as Noland's Store, around 1884 or '85. There are conflicting stories about subsequent ownership of the post. Frank McNitt, in his book *Indian Traders*, states that A. J. Ames and Jesse West bought the store when Noland moved to Navajo Springs. He also writes that Joseph Hefferman acquired the post from a man named Johnson about 1908, as told to McNitt by Mrs. John Ismay, Hefferman's daughter. One of Noland's daughters, Madeline McCrum, claims Noland was the sole owner of the post, and that he abandoned it after it was damaged during the disastrous San Juan River flood of 1911. It is possible that Hefferman operated the post for Noland but was not an owner.

In any case, a tragic incident occured at the post while Hefferman was the operator. Hefferman hired as his manager a bachelor named Charles Fritz who lived at the store alone. One evening two Navajos came to the store requesting assistance. Fritz let them in and was later found shot in the back and the store robbed. One of the two Native Americans was caught, put on trial for murder at Salt Lake City, and sentenced to ten years in prison.

Teec Nos Pos Trading Post★★

P. O. Box 940, Teec Nos Pos, AZ 86514, (928) 656-3224

Located on US 64, .1 mile east of the US 64/US 160 junction, which is 43 miles southwest of Cortez or 26 miles west of Shiprock, NM via US 64.

Description: *Renovated.* The current store, which was built in 1959, has been completely remodeled. It is a large, tan stucco building with a large parking area out front. The store sells groceries, videos, hardware,

and other general merchandise and has an excellent Indian Room with many rugs and other crafts and artifacts. The current owner recently started a restaurant in conjunction with the trading post called Cafe Teec (pronounced "tees"), which includes an outdoor patio.

History: Teec Nos Pos means "trees all around." The name applied to the original post which had large cottonwoods growing around it and was

Old Teec Nos Pos Trading Post at original site, 1912. (Farmington Museum, #46042)

located on a wash approximately two miles southwest of the present store. It was started in 1905 by Hambleton B. Noel in partnership with Hugh Currie. Noel was the first white man the Navajos permitted to establish a trading post in this section of the reservation. It was only through his friendship with Black Horse, a Navajo leader known for his hostility toward white men, that permission was gained to start the post. Black Horse was the unofficial chief of the northeastern part of the reservation. He presented an imposing figure, being a lean six foot five inches tall, and ruled his people with a firm hand. He, along with a band of about 200, were the only Navajos to escape the 1864 "Long Walk" to Bosque Redondo.

The original trading post burned in 1959 and was rebuilt the same year at its current site just prior to the final location of the Highway US 160. It was planned that the location of the new store would be at the junction of the Highways US 160 & US 64. However, there was a slight miscalculation. When the surveying was completed, the highway junction was slightly to the west of the new store's location.

The trading post has been in the Foutz family almost from its start in 1905. Noel, who suffered from tuberculosis, married Eva Foutz, a Farmington, New Mexico native. In 1913, he sold out to Progressive Mercantile, a partnership at that time composed of Burt and Sheldon Dustin and Al and June Foutz, Eva's relatives. Al's son Luff Foutz ran it starting around 1930 until his death from meningitis in 1939. Luff's brother Russell then ran the business. In 1949, ownership was taken over by Russell with his cousins, Jay and Loyd Foutz, and they operated the post until 1970. Bill Foutz, Russell's son, ran it from 1970 to 1982, at which time he opened the Foutz Trading Company in Shiprock. Russell again ran it from 1982 until 1994, with the help of a series of managers. In 1994, he turned it over to his daughter Kathleen, and her then husband John McCulloch, who is the current owner. Russell Foutz passed away in September, 2005.

An incident involving the Teec Nos Pos store occurred in the fall of 1907. Indian Superintendent Shelton issued an order that Navajo children of certain areas must attend the boarding school at Shiprock. Byalille, head man of a clan and an influential medicine man then living in the Aneth region north of Teec-nos-pos, met the order with open defiance. Fearing trouble, Shelton requested cavalry troops from Fort Wingate. Noel was forewarned by friendly Navajos that if Byalille was attacked by the troops he might rob Noel's store, burn it, and kill him. However, just before daylight the troops were able to surround Byalille's camp near Aneth and take fifteen or twenty prisoners. Two Navajos were killed after one of them shot at the troopers but missed. Byallille and eight other Navajos were sentenced to prison and released two years later.

Beclahbeto Trading Post*
Shiprock, NM 87420, (928) 656-3455

Located on US 64, 18 miles west of Shiprock, NM or 7.3 miles east of the US 64/US 160 junction.

Description: *Converted.* The current post is housed in a cement block structure that has recently been painted white with red and blue trim. The building is a small, self-service grocery store that also carries other general merchandise items needed by the local clientele, which is almost exclusively Navajo. Prior to its recent sale it functioned as a "full-service" trading post — trading for wool, sheep, and other items. It was similiar to an old fashioned grocery and general merchandise store, and its operation was in a transition stage between the old-

time trading post it once was and the modern self-service grocery store it became.

History: The original post was established by Billy Hunter in 1911. It is believed that Hunter built his post with material that washed down the San Juan River from Shiprock, New Mexico following the record 1911 flood. Biffle Morris took it over from Hunter and sold it to Hugh Foutz in 1924. The partnership of Russell Foutz and his cousins, Jay and Loyd Foutz, assumed ownership in 1951 with Jay and Loyd becoming the sole owners in 1969 until its recent sale to the current owner, Red Mesa Express. The original post, which was located on the old road to

Shiprock about one mile north of the current store, burned in 1953.The current post was rebuilt on the highway the following year. The old road is still present, but nothing remains of the old post. The area around the post is very attractive. Located at the north edge of the Carrizo mountains, it is a little higher in elevation than the surrounding country and its landscape includes many pinon and juniper trees. Baclabito (another spelling for the name) means "water under a ledge," and it is also the area where the Teec Nos Pos rug originates.

Red Mesa Trading Post*

HC 61, P. O. Box 38, Teec Nos Pos, AZ 86514, (928) 656-3261

Located on US 160, 15.7 miles west of the US 160/US 64 junction.

Description: *Converted.* The current store is in an attractive, well-maintained building constructed of painted cinder blocks and has an adjoining residence to the rear. It now functions more as a self-service convenience store than a trading post, selling gas and groceries, and also buying and selling a small amount of Native American arts and crafts.

History: The original post was located 2.7 miles due north of the present store, close to the Arizona-Utah state line. It was made of chiseled red sandstone and consisted of three rooms — a trading room, wareroom,

and an all-purpose living room. A dirt road leads to the site where ruins of the walls remain. The post was established in 1901 by Bob Martin, one of the few Navajos who operated a trading post at that time. Roscoe McGee, with partners Willard Stolworthy and Sheldon Dustin, bought it from Martin in 1932. Bradley Blair became a partner from 1945 until 1965 when Roscoe, his brother Jewel, and Jewel's son Lavoy became partners and assumed ownership. Lavoy subsequently bought out Roscoe and Jewel, and eventually sold the post to Thriftway in 1984, followed by Red Mesa Express. The current store was built by Roscoe McGee and Brad Blair in 1962 shortly after the new US 160 was completed.

Sweetwater Trading Post⋆

Located approximately 14 miles south of US 160 on NR (Navajo Route) 35, which leaves the highway across from Red Mesa Trading Post; from the highway go south for 12 miles to a 4-way intersection then right for two miles.

Description: *Abandoned.* The more recent trading post was housed in a prefab metal building. It was not much of a store, being a relatively small, plain structure with a very sparse interior. Since closing it has been greatly vandalized, and the building itself has been damaged beyond use. The original post was made of native sandstone and was located where the metal building currently stands. It was a much larger building which included the store and an adjoining residence. There was also a separate stone bunkhouse and a large barn.

History: The original post was established by Johnny Wade around 1911. Subsequent owners were Ace Palmer (1922), Ace Palmer and Roy Foutz (1929), Ace Palmer again (1935), Roscoe and Kelly McGee (1944), and Roscoe McGee and John Arrington (1964). Jay and Lloyd Foutz leased it in 1973 until they closed it in 1978. Shortly after the original post was closed David "Boots" Wagon (aka Wagner), a Navajo, tore it down and put up the replacement metal building. It was opened and closed a number of times under various managers, including Wilbur Martin and Sonny Gustamonte. The last lessee was Bob Garlinghouse, who closed it in 1996. There is not much to see as far as the post is concerned, but the remote location makes a visit to the area worthwhile.

Ace Palmer (on right) and son Richard in front of Sweetwater Trading Post, about 1939. (Photo courtesy of Fern Duckworth)

Johnny Arrington behind counter at Sweetwater Trading Post, about 1965. (Photo courtesy of Grace Herring)

Mexican Water Trading Post★

HC 61, P. O. Box 50, Teec Nos Pos, AZ 86514, (928) 691-1889

Located on US 160, .5 mile east of the US 160/US 191 junction.

Description: *Converted.* The place where Mexican Water is located has been described as "a spot of green in a pocket of red cliffs," due to the

small amount of moisture available in the area. The current store is made of cinder block construction and is very neat and well maintained. In addition to the store, a restaurant and laundromat are in separate buildings next to it. The post now functions as a convenience store, selling gas and groceries plus some hardware, auto supplies, and general merchandise. It also buys and sells a limited amount of Indian arts and crafts.

History: The post was established by Hambleton B. Noel in 1907. Subsequent owners included partners John Hunt and John Walker (1912), John Hunt and Charlie Ashcroft (1913), Charlie Ashcroft (1918), Harvey Gibson (1923), Harvey's son, Walter "Bud" Gibson (1934), Bob Smith (1946), Roscoe and Jewel McGee (1948), Don Reeves (1964), Morris Butts (1984), and finally the current owner, Red Mesa Express, in 2001.

The original post was located on the edge of an arroyo about four miles northwest of the present store. It washed out after a couple of years and was moved one-quarter mile east in 1910. It was moved again to its present location on the highway by the McGees in 1963. A modern Navajo Chapter House is now located where the original post once stood and is accessible via a gravel road which leaves the highway about 2.7 miles west of the present store. Nothing remains of the old posts at either of the previous sites. The name of the post in Navajo was Nakai Toh and a couple of translations are given concerning its meaning. One states that it means "traveler's water" or "where the travelers dug for water." Mormons, passing through the area, stopped and dug for water in a damp sandstone hill. The Navajos mistook them for Mexicans or Spanish, thus the name Mexican Water. Another version calls it the "water of the moving people" because the Wetherills supposedly stopped and dug for water in the area while passing through. A book written by Walter Gibson entitled *NakaiToh* is available and gives some interesting history and background on the old Mexican Water Trading Post.

OTHER ABANDONED TRADING POSTS

■ **Ute:** It is located on US 160, ten miles south of Cortez; the original post was located 1/2 mile west and then was moved to the present site in 1929. It was started by Bob Brice in the early 1900s, followed by Lewis Ismay (1920), Frank Pyle (1932), the Ute tribe (1947), Leonard Hatch & Frank Pyle (1957), Byron Pyle (1966), the Ute tribe again in 1977 and they converted it to a pottery store in 1989.

■ **Towaoc:** The last store was located next to Towaoc Post Office. The original post was started by Oen Noland in 1911 at Navajo Springs, three miles south of Towaoc and moved to Towaoc by Don Crawford in 1919. Other owners were Pete Schifferer, Werner Helms, and Francis Griswold. Frank and Bryon Pyle acquired it in 1949 and sold it to the Ute tribe in 1977. They closed it in 1982. Nothing remains.

■ **Wilson:** It was located fifteen miles west of Towaoc and seven miles north of old Aneth road. It was started by Billy Meadows about 1913; sold to Dick and Nora Wilson, and then closed in the early 1950s. Ruins remain.

■ **East McElmo (Hall Store):** It was located on McElmo Wash about four miles northwest of where old Aneth road crosses Marble Wash. It was started by Ern Hall about 1938 and closed after he died in 1947. Nothing remains.

■ **Mokie Jim:** It was located about 3/4 mile south and a little east of the Hall store. It was started by Jim Holly in the late 1920s. It was just a dugout in the hillside and only lasted a few years. Nothing remains.

■ **Tanner Mesa:** It was located on Tanner Mesa just north of the New Mexico state line and about ten miles east of US 491. It was started by

Joe Tanner in the early 1900s; sold to Frank Pyle and Jim Belmear in 1919; and closed in 1923. Some ruins remain.

■ **Hatch (Four Corners):** It was located about 3/4 mile south of US 160 where UT 41 joins it. It was started by Leonard Hatch and Frank Pyle in 1941; it was closed by Claude Hatch in 1949. Ruins remain.

■ **Meadows:** It was located on the San Juan River approximately twelve miles southeast of the Four Corners Monument. It was started by Billy Meadows in 1900 and closed around 1912. Nothing remains.

■ **Bluff:** It was located in Bluff, Utah at a current elementary school site. It was started in the early 1900s; Claude Powell took it over about 1928, and it burned down in 1936. Nothing remains.

■ **Dinnehotso:** It was located at the community of Dinnehotso. It was started by Charlie Ashcroft in 1924, followed by his son, Charles (1934), Vernon Bloomfield (1938), Roscoe & Jewel McGee and Walter Kennedy (1948), Walter Kennedy (1953), Bob Tanner (1982), and Phil Foutz (1988). The post was closed in 1994, and building demolished in 2000.

Chapter 2

Kayenta

Tuba T.P. 4/20/86 Az   Abraham L. Tucker

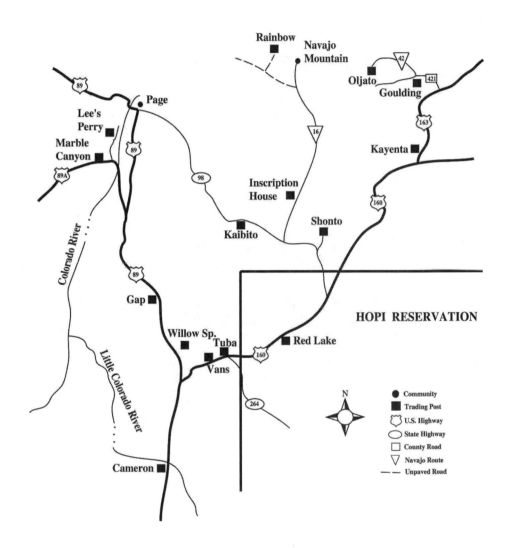

Kayenta Trading Post★★★
P. O. Box 1220, Kayenta, AZ 86033, (928) 697-3541

Located one block west of US 163 in Kayenta, Arizona. From the junction of US 160/US 163 go north 1.4 miles; turn left at the large "Kayenta Trading Post" sign.

Description: *Converted.* The current Kayenta Trading Post, which is located about 100 yards east of the original site, is housed in a large cinder block structure. Radio Shack occupies the south end of the same building. The newer facility currently operates as a super market and has not functioned as a trading post since 1987. Nothing remains of the original post, which was made of stone. A burnt out shell remains of the old Wetherill residence, which was a large L-shaped wooden building.

History: John Wetherill, along with a partner named Clyde Colville, established the post in 1910. At that time the post was located in a very remote part of the country, and Wetherill boasted that their post office was the farthest from a railroad of any in the U.S.. A second trading post was built by Wethcrill in 1932 a short distance from the original, which was then converted into a workshop and storage area. Wetherill died in 1944 and his wife Louisa and his partner Clyde Colville sold the trading post about a year later. There was some question as to whom it was sold; however, the Babbitt archives stored at the Northern Arizona University Cline Library show that Babbitt Bros.Trading Co. bought it in May 1945 and later sold it to James Ashcroft in July 1954. Colville died shortly after the Babbitts bought the post, and Louisa moved away. Bennett Hyde was the manager for at least part of the Babbitt ownership. The old Wetherill residence, in which lodging and meals were provided to many guests, was sold separately and was operated as a cafe and lodge until it burned in 1976.

In 1955, Reuben and Glenwood Heflin purchased the trading post from Ashcroft and the next year Glenwood sold his share of the post to his brother Reuben. Shortly after Reuben acquired it, he moved the trading post into a larger cinder block building built a short distance east of Wetherill's second post which was then and continues to be used for storage. In 1959-60, the Heflins built the Wetherill Inn motel which is located on the hill just above the current store. Mildred and Reuben sold both the trading post and the Inn to Elijah and Bradley Blair in 1966. Four enlargements to the store bring it to its current size. It ceased functioning as a trading post when the Blair's sold it and the motel to Gerold and Roland LaFonte in 1987. The LaFonte's subsequently sold the store in 1994 to the current owners, Ronnie and Melissa Biard.

John Wetherill, along with his brother Richard, discovered the Mesa Verde ruins and developed a keen interest in archaeology. He guided many exploratory trips to archaeological sites in the area, including Rainbow Bridge and Betatakin Ruin. The Wetherill home was visited by many famous guests such as President Theodore Roosevelt, Western writer Zane Grey, and numerous well-known archaeologists.

Goulding Trading Post★★★★
P. O. Box 360001, Monument Valley, UT 84536, (435) 727-3231

Located on CR 421, 1.5 miles west of US 163; this junction is 24 miles north of Kayenta, AZ.

Description: *Converted.* The old trading post no longer functions as such. However, it has been fully restored, depicting how the Gouldings lived when their home served as the trading post. Downstairs is the old store that is a replica of the original trading post. The upstairs contains the living quarters and a museum about the history of the Goulding family with displays of Native American artifacts from the area and memorabilia of the Gouldings. There is also a room dedicated to the movies that have been made in Monument Valley, the first of which was the classic *Stagecoach* in 1939 starring John Wayne. In addition to the rustic old trading post, there is a modern motel, restaurant, and an outstanding Indian arts and crafts store, all located in a remarkably beautiful setting of tall buttes and mesas.

History: The original post was started by Harry Goulding in a tent in 1923. Monument Valley contained a portion of the Paiute Reservation known as the Paiute Strip and the State of Utah offered to trade the Paiute tribe more fertile land to the north for land in Monument Valley, which they accepted. Shortly after, the Gouldings laid claim to 640 acres of the state owned land at the base of Tsay-Kissi Mesa (Big Rock Door Mesa) at a cost of $320, set up their tents and a makeshift counter, and began

Harry Goulding standing by his trading post, about 1960. (Photo courtesy of Ronnie Biard)

trading. Goulding built the two-story stone building, currently housing the museum, and moved into it in 1928. He sold the property to Knox College of Illinois in 1963. They in turn sold it to Gerold and Roland LaFonte, the current owners, in 1981. The trading post was designated a State Historical Site in 1989.

Harry Goulding was responsible for bringing Hollywood to Monument Valley. Goulding wanted to help the local Paiutes and Navajos, destitute at the time, with some form of employment. He went to Hollywood and persuaded movie director John Ford to come to Monument Valley by showing him photos of the area. He practically camped in his office until Ford agreed to meet with him. Ford was very impressed with what he saw and agreed to move to the area for the shooting of *Stagecoach*. Thus started the production of a number of western movies in Monument Valley, including *Wagon Master, My Darling Clementine, Rio Grande, Fort Apache, She Wore a Yellow Ribbon, The Searchers, Sargent Rutledge,* and *Cheyenne Autumn.*

Oljato Trading Post★★★★
P. O. Box 360416, Monument Valley, UT, 84536, (435) 727-3210

> *From Monument Valley junction go west on CR 421 for 1.7 miles; turn right onto CR 410 (NR 42) for 10 miles to trading post at end of pavement.*

Description: *Closed.* Oljato (or "Moonlight Water") is currently closed, but hopefully will reopen in the near future. It is one of the few remaining trading posts that have retained their authenticity. The current building, though not the original, was built in 1921 and is made of stone with a low roof supported by vegas (large wooden beams). The interior still resembles the old-time posts with the bullpen arrangement and high counters. The back room has the original stone fireplace and floor and contains many artifacts collected by the previous traders at the post. When last open, the post carried on trading and sold rugs, baskets, pottery, and jewelry in addition to the groceries and general merchandise needed by the local Navajo clientele. The post is listed on the National Register of Historic Places. It is a remote post located off the beaten track, but the road to it is a beautiful drive.

History: John Wetherill, with Clyde Colville as a partner, started the post in 1906 in a tent on Moonlight Wash. A year later they moved one mile downstream and built a crude structure made of stone, juniper logs and adobe with a low dirt covered roof for the store, and an adjoining log residence. Wetherill had to convince Hoskinini, a local Navajo leader who was very hostile to white men and whose home camp was nearby, to give him permission to remain in the area. Wetherill closed the post in 1910 and moved to Kayenta. The old post remained empty for several years and was eventually burned down. All that remains are a number of short juniper logs that were buried upright in the ground and show the outline of part of the building. This site is located 1.6 miles southeast

Remains of original Oljato Trading Post.

of the current store and about 100 yards east of the road. In 1921, Jim Hefferman built the current post and after his death in 1926 his widow sold it to John Taylor. Jim Pierson bought it from Taylor in 1936 and two years later sold it to O. J. "Stokes" Carson. Shortly after, Stokes sold it to his daughter and son-in-law, Mildred and Reuben Heflin. They sold it to Stokes' cousin Fred Carson in 1945, who in turn sold it back to Stokes in 1948. Another of Stokes' daughters and son-in-law, Chin and Ed Smith, bought it in 1958. Their daughter, Wynona "Wy" Townsend, took it over in 1986 until the last owner, Evelyn Yazzie Jansen, bought it in 1991.

Shonto Trading Post★★★★
P.O. Box 7713, Shonto, AZ 86054, (928) 672-2320

> *From US 160 go north six miles on AZ 198 to NR 221;*
> *turn right for four miles then right again for .6 mile*
> *down to the canyon bottom.*

Description: *Original.* This is another of the few remaining trading posts that are still authentic. It has the added attraction of being located in a unique and beautiful setting at the bottom of Ten-Mile Canyon, a deep canyon with great buttes and rock formations rising hundreds of feet from the canyon floor. The early road into the canyon was extremely rough and hazardous and was described as the "roughest damn half-mile in America." In its earlier days, Shonto (Navajo for "Sunshine Water") consisted of an L-shaped store built in the stockade style of upright logs plastered with mud and with adjoining living quarters made of red sandstone. There were also adobe covered storage buildings, plus assorted wooden corrals. The store and residence have since been enlarged using boards and cement blocks. Current outbuildings include a wool barn and a shed for weighing and storing wool and pinyon nuts. The corrals are no longer in use and the guest hogans are used for storage. Directly across from the store is an attractive park-like area with numerous large cottonwood trees.

History: The post was established in 1912 by Joe Lee in partnership with John Wetherill. They started the post in a tent and later moved it into a wooden structure. C. D. Richardson bought the cabin-type store in 1914 and began constructing the first permanent stone buildings. He traded it to the Babbitt Brothers in 1928 and they were followed by Harry Rorick and wife Elizabeth Hegemann (1930); Reuben Heflin (1945); Sam Drolet and Willard Leighton (1958); Sam Drolet and Willard's widow, Marie (1960); Sam's son, Raymond Drolet (1986) with Marie Leighton's daughters, Pamela Evans and Betty Epperson, as partners (Raymond had been the manager since 1972), and the current owner, Jed Foutz in 1996.

The area around the post and north to Navajo Mountain is the location where a small band of Navajo "long hairs" took refuge in order to keep from being taken captive by Kit Carson and forced on the Long Walk to Fort Sumner in 1864. The current Navajos in this area are still known for their more traditional nature.

Inscription House Trading Post★★★
PMB 5300, Tonalea, AZ 86044, (928) 672-2651

> *From US 160 go north 12 miles on AZ 98, then turn right and go seven miles on NR 16.*

Description: *Original.* The original stone trading post is still in use selling hardware, tack, auto supplies, chainsaws, hats, saddles, kerosene, and other general merchandise; and it retains the authentic trading post appearance and atmosphere. In 1997, a new, larger metal building was constructed next door, which functions as a modern grocery store. The post still does some trading for wool, sheep, rugs, and blankets with the local Navajo customers.

History: S. I. Richardson established Inscription House in 1926. The first store was made of wood and was replaced by the present stone building in 1929. Richardson remained in business there for the next twenty-eight years before selling it in 1954 to Stokes Carson and his son-in-law Ruben Heflin, with Carson later buying Heflin out. After Stokes' death in 1974, at the age of eighty-eight, his granddaughter Wy and her husband Al Townsend, acquired it with Virginia Smith as a partner. The present owner, M. L. Townsend, took it over in 1988.

In addition to the trading post, Richardson built cabins for guests and ran pack trips to Rainbow Bridge and the Ancestral Puebloan ruins in the surrounding country. Inscription House is the name of a cliff

Loading sacks of wool at Inscription House Trading Post, 1960s. (Photo courtesy of Raymond Drolet)

dwelling in Neetsin Canyon to the west of the trading post. The area around Inscription House is known for storm pattern rugs and saddle blankets.

Rainbow Lodge Trading Post★★

From US 160 go north 12 miles on AZ 98; turn right onto NR 16 and go 32 miles; take left-hand fork off NR 16, go 4.6 miles and turn right for 2.3 miles to site; last 1.5 miles are extremely rough and require four-wheel drive.

Description: *Abandoned.* The original main building, which contained the store and living quarters, was made of red sandstone with a roof of

packed clay over peeled poles. There was also a guest house and cabins which were used to house guests making pack trips to Rainbow Bridge. A log barn and pole corrals were located below in the timber "far enough to keep the flies away from the lodge." Adjacent to the store was a lean-to warehouse, partially constructed of boards from Arbuckles Coffee packing crates. Due to the remoteness, the warehouse and store were crammed with merchandise each fall before the snows came so as to have enough supplies to last until spring. All that remains of these fine stone buildings is an outline of the foundations showing where they once were located.

History: S. I. Richardson established the trading post and lodge in 1924 and sold out to his brother and partner Hubert in 1926. Stanton Borum managed the store for Hubert, followed by his brother-in-law, Billy

Wilson, who later bought it with the late Senator Barry Goldwater as a partner. The lodge burned in 1951, while Wilson and Ted Hollaway owned it. Miles Hedrick rebuilt it, and it finally closed around 1957 and was subsequently torn down.

Kaibito Trading Post★
P. O. Box 1410, Kaibito, AZ 86053, (928) 673-3453

> *Located on NR 6331 (new paved section) .6 mile in from AZ 98; this junction is approximately 34 miles south of Page, AZ.*

Description: *Converted.* The current store is housed in an attractive, light tan cinder block building with a flat roof and dark brown trim on the upper part. It is primarily a modern supermarket selling groceries plus other general merchandise and no longer functions as a trading post. The original trading post was located on the old part of NR 6331, .4 mile past the Chapter House, which is .4 mile in from AZ 98. This junction off AZ 98 is about 1.5 miles east of the main turn-off to Kaibito. Ruins of the trading post and other buildings are still present.

History: The original trading post was established by C. D. Richardson in 1914. In 1921, Richardson sold it to Earl Morris who had it for two years and then sold it to Hubert Richardson, C. D.'s brother. Hubert and his son Bud ran it until 1966 when they sold it to Alvin Kerley. Kerley remodeled the store in 1970, at which time it ceased functioning as a traditional trading post. He sold it in 1975 to Bob Redd. By 1987 its location proved to be too remote and isolated from the main population of the community. Redd closed the old store, built the current building, and moved into it. The old post was torn down a year later. Stan Patterson, the current owner, has managed both stores since 1980 and became the owner in 1990.

Red Lake Trading Post★★★★
P. O. Box 330, Tonalea AZ 86044, (928) 283-5194

Located on US 160, 22.4 miles east of Tuba City.

Description: *Original.* The current building, although not the original, is quite old and one of the few really authentic trading posts still in existence. It is a two story building constructed of stone with the upper level, which is used as a residence, originally made of wood from

Arbuckles Brothers coffee crates. Arbuckles coffee was very popular and sold in trading posts all over the reservation in the early days. Wood from its crates was used for every conceivable purpose including sheds, counters, shelves, wall covering, storage boxes, baby beds, or just about anything made of wood. The ground floor consists of the store and an adjoining wareroom that is lined with wood from the Arbuckles crates with old names written on them. Some changes and improvements have been made to the post over the years, but it has not been modernized and definitely retains the old-time trading post atmosphere. At one time back in the late '30s a string of rustic cabins was put in for the traveling motorist, but they, along with many of the other original buildings, have been abandoned and removed. The current owner, Lorenzo Fowler, grew up in the area and says that the majority of his customers are local Navajos. He wants to

Old Red Lake Trading Post, showing dried up lake bed in foreground, 1949.
(Museum of New Mexico, #46040)

run the store in the old traditional way as much as possible and is happy to show visitors around the old, historic interior.

History: The original Red Lake trading post was a log and adobe hut started by Joseph Lee in 1881. George McAdams, who had started a post on Rabbit Mesa in 1879, five miles north of Tuba City, joined forces with Joe Lee in 1885 and built a new post on what apppeared to be a dry lake bed. However, two years later the spring run-off filled the lake (which no longer exists), and they were forced to move the post to higher ground where it now stands. It originally consisted of a stockade-type structure made of juniper logs with four rooms and a dirt roof. In 1888, the post was sold to Sam "Ditt" Dittenhoffer. Two years later, during a poker game at Red Lake, Dittenhoffer was shot and killed in an argument over a woman. The story goes that on one of his trips to Flagstaff he became involved with Mrs. Mathews, a widow from Flagstaff, and took her back to the trading post. A few days later a stranger showed up who was another one of her admirers, got into an argument during a poker game, and shot Dittenhoffer. Dittenhoffer, who purchased all of his supplies from the Babbitt Brothers Trading Company on credit, was so in debt to them at the time of his death that they were forced to take over the trading post in order to protect their investment. This started the Babbitts in the actual ownership of trading posts, eventually totaling nineteen. In 1891, Samuel S. Preston became a managing partner and built the present two story stone building. In 1895, McAdams took back half-interest in the post with the Babbitts as partners, and eventually sold out to them in 1904. The Babbitts continued to own the post until they closed it in 1987. It was reopened by the current owner, Lorenzo Fowler, in 1991.

Back in the late 1800s Red Lake was probably one of the most colorful and active posts on the reservation. The rugged canyon country nearby became a hiding place for renegades from as far east as New Mexico, and protection became a necessity. When McAdams owned the post he constructed the countertops around the bull pen so they could be raised to form a barricade or fortress for his clerks. They could be raised in a flash with one hand while reaching for a weapon with the other. Indians were constantly passing by enroute from the northern part of the reservation to the southern, and a trail crossing into central Arizona from Colorado and Utah was located nearby. Herds of cattle and flocks of sheep came down this route to be sold at Prescott and around Phoenix. Returning stockmen stopped at Red Lake to visit and take part in poker games, and the post became, for lack of better terminology, one of the wild and wooly centers for both cowboys and Indians. In more recent years, the trading post was used as a movie location. In 1992, scenes for the movie *The Dark Wind*, based on the novel by Tony Hillerman, were filmed there. Zane Grey made periodic visits to the post and wrote the novel *Rainbow Trail* while staying at Red Lake.

Tuba Trading Post★★★
P. O. Box 247, Tuba City, AZ 86045, (928) 283-5441

Located in Tuba City, one mile north of US 160.

Description: *Renovated.* The trading post is still housed in the original building, which is an attractive two-story octagon shaped structure constructed of native blue-gray sandstone. Logs for the roof of the original post were hauled in from the San Francisco mountains. The main building has been converted into an arts and crafts store with a small convenience store adjoining the west side. Its function as a traditional trading post has diminished in recent years. In addition to the

authentic Indian arts and crafts store, there is a motel, restaurant, and RV park. The trading post is listed on the National Register of Historic Places.

History: The original post, which was a wooden one-story, rectangular building, was established in 1885 by Charles H. Algert. He sold it to the Babbitt Brothers in 1905. Samuel Preston, who had originally worked for Algert, was retained by the Babbitts as a managing partner. Around 1920, Preston designed and built the present hogan-shaped building as an addition to the original store. Jot Stiles was another partner from around 1926 until 1930. Over time, several additions and improvements have been made to the building, with major remodeling in 1955 drastically changing the interior appearance. Around 1986 the Babbitt Brothers Trading Company undertook a project to undo the changes made in 1955 and restored the interior with spectacular results. The Babbits sold the trading post to Navajo Nation Hospitalities, Inc., in November 1999.

Tuba City was established by Erastus Snow in 1878 and named after Hopi headman Tuuvi (Too-vah), which was misspelled and pronounced Tuba by Anglos. He gave the first fourteen Mormon families in the area a place to build their town, and they named it in his honor. The Navajo reservation was enlarged around Tuba City in 1884, and the federal government bought out the Mormon interest in 1902 for $45,000. Within a year it became part of the reservation. The trading post was often visited by famous movie stars, politicians, and scientists. President Theodore Roosevelt was a guest of the Preston family in 1913. Western novelist Zane Grey often visited the trading post, and films based on his books were shot around the Tuba City area. The Storm pattern rug was developed in the Tuba City area.

Van Trading Company★★
P. O. Box 7, Tuba City, AZ 86045, (928) 283-5343

Located on US 160, 1.5 miles west of Tuba City.

Description: *Converted.* The current store is a large, modern cinder-block building that sells gas, groceries, dry goods, and other general merchandise. It also sells rugs and other Indian arts and crafts, still does limited trading, and is the only trading post on the reservation that still takes pawn.

History: The original store, called Kerley's Trading Post, was started by John Kerley in 1921. The old building is still located behind the present store. Prior to establishing the post, Kerley managed Babbitts' Tuba Trading Post and then ran a small trading post of his own nearby from 1916 to 1921. He decided he wanted to get out of town and moved to what became known as Kerley's Valley, where he started his new post. His brother Alvin Kerley eventually took over the post and then sold it to Warner VanKeuren in 1954. It became known as Van's Trading Post. When VanKeuren's son Danny bought it in 1982, he built the current building and moved the store into it, renaming it Van Trading Company.

Cameron Trading Post★★★
P. O. Box 339, Cameron, AZ 85200, (800) 338-7385

Located on US 89, 54 miles north of the Flagstaff.

Description: *Renovated.* Cameron Trading Post is a unique blend of traditional trading customs and modern-day commerce. The early trading post building is still in use, though it has been enlarged and

remodeled. A major portion has become tourist oriented and includes an outstanding Indian arts & crafts and curio shop. There is also a portion, although it has become smaller in recent years, that carries groceries and dry goods needed by its local Navajo customers. The Navajos still trade wool, livestock, and craft items for groceries and other merchandise. There is also a restaurant, motel, and art gallery. All the major buildings, including several improvements and enlargements, are constructed of cut native sandstone similiar to earlier construction material.

History: The original store was built by Samuel Preston in 1910 during the construction of the suspension bridge across the Little Colorado River. It was operated by his wife while he freighted materials for the new bridge. The post was a small, plain structure made of wood and corrugated tin. Shortly after the bridge was completed in 1912, Preston closed the post and returned to Tuba City. In 1916, Hubert Richardson built a fairly large wooden store near the west end of the new bridge, which he called Little Colorado Trading Post. He constructed additional sandstone buildings in the late 1920s. He renamed the post Cameron after his friend territorial Senator Ralph Cameron, who was influential in having the old one-lane bridge built over the river gorge. The bridge served travelers until 1958 when the current bridge was constructed next to it. Following Hubert's retirement in 1966, the post was leased to Gilbert Ortega. In 1977, Joe Atkinson, Hubert Richardson's grand-nephew, purchased Cameron and currently co-owns the post with employees. After taking it over he added the restaurant and refurbished the motel. The original hotel and trader's quarters are now the art gallery. Over the years the post has hosted many prominent guests, including Zane Grey, Errol Flynn, and John Wayne.

Willow Springs Trading Post★★★

*Located off US 89, 6.2 miles north of the US 160/US 89
junction; turn right at mile post 487 onto NR 23, go .4
mile across Hamblin Wash and turn left onto dirt road
for .4; site is about 200 yards east of the road.*

Description: *Abandoned.* The remains of the stone walls of a large
structure are still standing. They are about two feet thick, twelve feet tall
and sixty feet long. This was probably the main building, which may have
housed the trading post and wareroom plus living quarters. The spring

itself sits high on
a rocky bench in
the cliffs to the
east. Water from
the spring must
have flowed close
by the trading
post since old pictures show large trees growing around it. Although the
remains may be limited, the location and history of the old post make it
an extremely interesting place to visit.

History: The first trading post was built by John Bigalowe in 1876 and
closed a few years later. George McAdams, in partnership with Babbitt
Brothers, reestablished the post in 1885. Samuel Preston took it over in
1895. In 1905, Preston married and returned to Tuba City to again work
for the Babbitts. They then took over Willow Springs which they closed
in 1915.

On the left side of the road, shortly before reaching its end at a
Navajo residence, is a low hill with a pile of large rocks which have
dates as early as 1878 inscribed on them, along with the names of
pioneer settlers who traveled through the area on the old Honeymoon
Trail. This trail was used by early-day Mormons to reach the newly
completed Mormon temple in St. George, Utah, where they went to
solemnize their civil marriages. Several trading posts were established
along the trail to provide food and supplies to travelers as well as trade
items for the Navajos. Other trading posts along the trail, in addition
to Willow Springs, were Echo Cliffs, White Mesa, Cedar Ridge, and
Lee's Ferry.

The Gap Trading Post★★★
Cameron, AZ 86020, (928) 283-8932

Located on US 89, 17 miles north of its junction with US 160.

Description: *Renovated.* The current store is located in a rustic native stone building with vegas protruding out the front. The store has not been greatly modernized, and the interior still has an old-time flavor. Although it still continues some of the functions of an old trading post, its main operation is as a small grocery and general merchandise store. It also has a good selection of Navajo rugs and other artifacts. The name of the post refers to a large break in the Echo Cliffs to the east, over which a road and several power transmission lines now pass.

History: The early history of this post is uncertain, as a couple of conflicting versions have been given. According to an article written by Gladwell Richardson entitled *Bonanza in the Ghost Post* (1966), the first store at The Gap was started in an old wooden building on Hamblin Wash by the copper mining company. In 1916, C. D. Richardson bought the mining company building at a sheriff's sale and opened his post in it. He sold the post in 1921, and the following year it was sold to Joe Lee and J. C. Brown. When the highway was rerouted and paved, they built a stone building across the road and remained in business until a fire destroyed the building in 1938. It was subsequently rebuilt at its present location.

Another article entitled *Traders at the Gap* by Mora McManis Brown (1940) seems to support this version. Ms. Brown interviewed J. C. Brown (no relation) in Flagstaff, Arizona in 1940. According to the article, the post was started in the copper mining company's old commissary building. Brown acquired an interest in the trading post in 1922 from Joe Lee, great grandson of John Doyle Lee, and sold his interest in 1936. The article also mentions that the old post was destroyed by fire and replaced with a stone building, and that J. P. O'Farrell was the post's operator when the article was written in 1940.

More recent owners of the Gap Trading Post included Ralph and Madelene Cameron in 1949, B. B. Bonner in 1953, Jess Walker and Lark Washburn in 1957, Troy Washburn in 1959, and Thriftway Corp. in 1986. Thriftway subsequently sold to Giant Industries. The current owner is Red Mesa Express.

Lee's Ferry Trading Post★★★

*Located about five miles off US 89; turnoff is one mile
past Navajo Bridge.*

Description: *Abandoned.* An old stone building that was originally built as a fort and later housed a trading post is still standing. The site is a National Monument

History: John Doyle Lee arrived at the site on the Colorado River that became known as Lee's Ferry in December, 1869. Lee, who had five wives, lived in exile at the site after taking part in the "Mountain

Meadows Massacre" of 1857, in which sixty-seven members of the Fancher party were killed by Paiutes and Mormons led by Lee. He was eventually captured in 1874 and executed by firing squad on March 23, 1877, at the site of the massacre.

Lee established a ferry shortly after he arrived, assisted Navajos and Paiutes in crossing the Colorado River, and immediately started trading with them. The ferry was the only river crossing for hundreds of miles and remained in use until Navajo Bridge was completed in 1929. While operating the trading post, Lee and his family lived close by at a place he called Lonely Dell. The trading post was operated by Jacob Hamblin part of the time from 1872 until 1877. The Mormon Church bought the ferry from Lee's widow in 1877 and closed the trading post. In 1879, a small stone fort was built for protection, and after it was no longer needed, it was used as a trading post. Several men traded there sporadically until the Mormon Church sold the ferry to the Grand Cattle Company in 1909. The cattle company subsequently sold it to Coconino County in 1916.

Lee's Ferry, 1873. First ferry used on Upper Colorado River. (Arizona Historical Society, #76695)

Marble Canyon Lodge & Trading Post
Marble Canyon, AZ 86036, (928) 355-2225

Located on US 89, one-quarter mile past Lee's Ferry turnoff, 42 miles from Page, AZ.

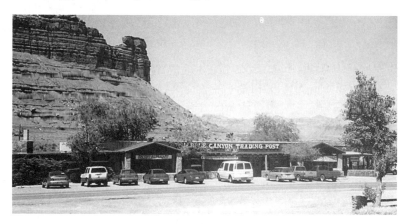

Description: *Converted.* The site presently consists of the main lodge, dining room, trading post which functions as a curio shop and arts & crafts store, and several rock cottages located across the highway.

History: The original trading post and lodge were built by David Crockett Lowrey in 1928 and operated by his son Buck Lowrey until 1937, when Lorenzo Hubbell, Jr. acquired it. Kyle Bales bought it in 1950. Mr. Bales died in 1959, and since that time the lodge has been owned and operated by his daughter Jane Foster and her three sons, Steven Knisely, David Foster, and Don Foster.

OTHER ABANDONED TRADING POSTS

■ **Warren:** The post was located .3 mile west of Kayenta trading post on the south side of the road just before the pavement ends. H. K. Warren started it in 1927; Babbitts acquired it in the 1930s with Warren retaining one-third interest. They assumed full ownership in 1945 and closed it in 1978. Nothing remains.

■ **Tsegi:** It was located on US 160, eleven miles west of Kayenta. H. T. Donald, a Navajo, started the post in 1945 and sold it to Jim Porter around 1960. It was later resold and then closed around 1980. The building was recently torn down and only a pile of rubble remains.

■ **Navajo Mountain:** The post was located at end of NR 16, thirty-seven miles north of AZ 98. Established by Ray Dunn in 1932. Alvin Kerley operated it in the late 1940s, followed by Ralph and Madelene Cameron in 1953. Dick Johnson acquired it in 1983 and closed it in 1993. The trading post was housed in an attractive stone building which is still standing and in fair condition. It was located on the lower edge of Navajo Mountain, one of the more remote parts of the Navajo Reservation.

■ **Cow Springs:** It was located on US 160, 46.6 miles east of Tuba City. Several trading posts were operated briefly in the Cow Springs area. The original post was built by George McAdams in 1882. Ben Williams operated the store from 1895 to 1898, and Fred Volz ran a post close by from 1894 to 1896. Another store, built by the Babbitts in 1924, was located one mile north. They closed it and built the most recent store in 1956, prior to completion of the new highway (US 160). They closed it for good in 1991. The building is still standing, but it is in poor condition.

■ **Blue Canyon:** It was located fifteen miles south of Red Lake Trading Post on NR 21. The original post was started by Jonathan Williams in 1882 and closed in 1886. Lorenzo Hubbell ran it for one year in 1886-87; C. H. Algert operated the post for a few years around 1902; Claude & Hubert Richardson reopened a post in 1913 in leased government school buildings and closed it in 1921; Lorenzo Hubbell, Jr. ran a seasonal post in 1927. Only a few ruins remain. The post occupied one of the more remote areas of the reservation.

■ **Nava-Hopi:** The site was not located. It's approximate location was at the west end of Main Street in Tuba City. It was started by C. D. Richardson in 1925; the Babbitt brothers acquired it in 1928. It was housed in a two-story, stone building; the government eventually bought the building and then tore it down in 1947.

■ **Western Navajo, Bell, and McAdams:** These are three old trading posts that existed in the Tuba City area, about which little is known other than their names. The Western Navajo and Bell posts were both owned by Babbitt Brothers; the McAdams store was started by George

McAdams and run by his brother, J. H. McAdams, from 1896 to 1898 when he left to fight in the Spanish-American War.

■ **C. H. Algert:** Algert's original store was located in Tuba City until 1903 when it was moved to Fruitland, New Mexico. It operated as the C. H. Algert Company, a wholesale trading supply store. After a few years it was sold to Al Foutz, Wilard Stolworthy, and Bert and Sheldon Dustin. It became the Progressive Mercantile Company.

■ **Stone:** It was located in the vicinity of Tuba City. Originally started by Thomas Hubbell (no relation to Lorenz Hubbell) in 1871, it was sold to Ed Stone in 1879. In 1887, Lott Smith seized the post by force and moved the merchandise to the store of the United Order, a Mormon cooperative.

■ **Reservoir Canyon:** It was located in the Tuba City area, built by Joe Tanner around 1879, and operated until 1914. Nothing remains.

■ **Echo Cliffs and White Mesa:** They were located north of Willow Springs; actual sites not located. George McAdams and C. H. Algert had Echo Cliffs from 1890 to 1920. Little else is known about them other than that they were at one time owned by the Babbitt Brothers.

■ **Cedar Ridge:** Located on US 89, seven miles north of The Gap Trading Post. It was originally located three miles southeast and was started by C. H. Algert in 1890. Babbitt Brothers acquired it in 1895 with John Kerley having one-half interest, and they moved it in 1912. Earl Boyer ran it in 1921; Jay Powell managed it from 1948 until around 1960; it closed about 1990 and was subsequently torn down. Nothing is left but a cement slab.

■ **Bitter Springs:** It was located at the junction of US 89 and Alternate US 89. Not much is known about it other than it was started in the early 1920s. Nothing remains.

■ **Copper Mine:** It is located just off NR 20, 18.4 miles south of Page, then west on NR 6210 for .3 mile. It was started by Bennett Hyde in 1931, followed by Claude Thompson in the early 1940s, Coit "Pat" Patterson in 1955, and Thel Black in 1977. Black's wife Anna Jean subsequently took it over and then closed it in 1988. The buildings, which were originally part of the mining operation, remain, but they are in poor condition. They include a stone residence and adjoining trading post, two dwellings, a guest hogan, a large metal warehouse, and a metal garage.

Chapter 3

Chaco Canyon

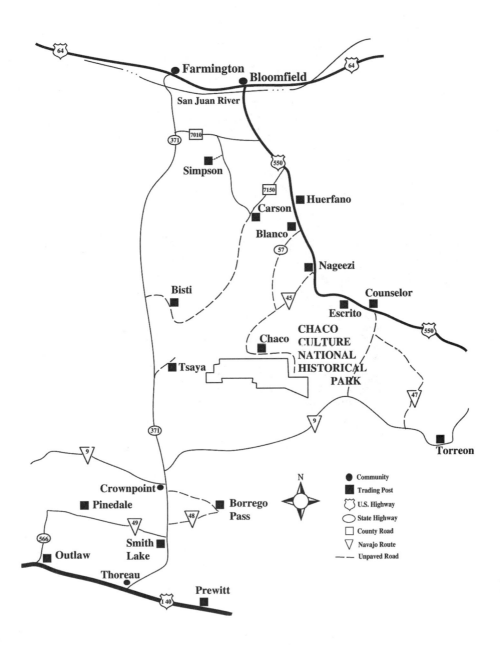

Carson Trading Post★★★★

P. O. Box 490, Bloomfield, NM 87413, (505) 325-3914

> *Go 12.5 miles south of Bloomfield, NM on US 550, then west 6.7 miles on CR 7150 (NR 5) to its junction with CR 7300; the post is on the left on CR 7300.*

Description: *Original.* This trading post is one you have to see to believe. It takes the prize for unaltered authenticity. It is still in the original building and very little change or renovation has been made to the post's stone exterior. Take away the soda machine and ice box from out front and it would appear much as it was when Stokes Carson first started it. The inside also appears to have changed little other than from wear and the ravages of time. It has been rearranged somewhat to facilitate more modern methods of handling and selling merchandise, but it is still quite authentic, maintaining the old bullpen arrangement.

History: The post was established in 1918 by O. J. "Stokes" Carson. Stokes' son-in-law, Sam Drolet, took it over around 1950 and was followed by his son, Raymond Drolet, in 1986. Since 1990, Bob Garlinghouse has leased it from Raymond and is the current operator. Nick and George Mayer, who originally traded out of a tent at the site, started the foundation for the current post, part of which they hewed out of the sandstone bedrock. The building was completed by Stokes

Last wagon loads of wool from Carson Trading Post going to Farmington market. (Photo courtesy of Raymond Drolet)

Pack train leaving Carson Trading Post with supplies for another store in the Bisti area, 1932. (Photo courtesy of Raymond Drolet)

when he took it over. The original post was a small, two room stone building. Later a storeroom and living quarters were built. A barn, other out buildings, and corrals were added; and, in 1920, a gas pump was installed. The post still does limited trading with local Navajos and has been in continuous operation except for one short period of two years in 1987. Next to Hubbell Trading Post, Carson is one of the most authentic posts on or around the reservation.

Huerfano Trading Post

The post had five different locations, the last located on the east side of US 550, 22 miles south of Bloomfield, NM.

Description: *Abandoned.* Only a few relics and some foundation stones for the building remain at the original site. A stone building and hogan are left where O. J. Carson moved the post to the highway. Since the store closed at its last location on the east side of US 550 it has sat abandoned and has gradually deteriorated from vandalism and salvage of materials. Now only rubble remains.

History: The original trading post was established by Leo Lampton in 1913. It consisted of a tiny, solitary store located close to the foot of Huerfano Butte. Lampton sold the post in 1923 to Ralph Townsend, who moved it two years later to a spring about a mile east of present Highway US 550. He owned it for ten years and then sold it to Glen Swire. In 1936, O. J. "Stokes" Carson bought it from Swire, and he and his family ran it until 1952. Shortly after acquiring it, Stokes moved the post to the south, to a small wash about two miles from Huerfano Butte. When the current Highway US 550 was paved, he again moved the store up to the roadside on the west side of the highway. There he built a small stone trading post and barn, plus a couple hogans for visitors, as was the custom in those days. He sold the post to A. M. "Red" Bloomfield who moved it to its last location across the highway. Bloomfield was followed by Danny Brimhall in 1967, Jack Richards in 1973, and David Randelman in 1975. Randelman closed the post for good in 1976.

Blanco Trading Post★★
12341 So. Hwy. US 550, Bloomfield, NM 87413, (505) 632-1219

Located on US 550, 28 miles south of Bloomfield, NM.

Description: *Renovated.* The post is still in the original building and has had only limited renovation. The building is constructed of adobe with a stucco overlay. It is attractive, and well maintained, and has the appearance of the typical modern-day trading post. It has been in continuous operation since it was established, except for a brief period in 2000. The store sells mainly groceries and gas, but also buys and sells sheep, hay, wood, coal, tack, and old pawn. The post does considerable tourist business since it is located close to Chaco Culture National Historic Park. The current owner recently opened a small cafe inside the store, and there is an interesting Indian Room stocked with quality Navajo rugs and other crafts and artifacts.

History: The post was established by C. J. Burnham and Wilford "Tabby" Brimhall around 1911. It was operated by Myrl Harper from 1952 to 1958. Subsequent owners included Leonard Taft and Harold McDonald (1958), Harold and Jane McDonald (1967), Jane McDonald (1988), and Bruce Burch (1990). Mr. Burch was killed in a vehicle accident in 1995, and his wife Julie took over the store ownership. Between 1998 and 2000 she made a couple unsuccessful attempts at leasing it, until her son and his wife, Justin and Savannah Higgins, took over the operation. An unfortunate incident occurred at the post in 1988 when one of the former owners, Harold McDonald, was killed — stabbed in the back by a Navajo in a robbery.

Nageezi Trading Post★

P. O. Box 7, Negeezi, NM 87037, (505) 632-7106

Located on US 550, 36 miles south of Bloomfield, NM.

Description: *Closed.* The old building is still in good condition with two additions — a large metal structure on one side and a cement block room on the other. The front of the main store has been covered with the same green siding used on the metal addition. There are also a couple of old barns and a corral out back. The store operated mainly as a small self-service gas and grocery store and has not functioned as a traditional trading post for several years. A bed and breakfast was also operated in the house next door.

History: The post was established by Jim Brimhall in the late 1930s and was originally located about two miles due south of the present store. It was bought by Jim McEwen in 1951 and subsequently moved to its present location. It was sold to Harry and Juanita Batchelor in 1971. Don Batchelor, Harry's son, took it over in 1990 and operated it until he closed it in 1997. He died in 2005, and it is reported that his mother, who still owns the store, has plans to reopen it in the near future. A Post Office was established at the post in 1941, and a new Post Office building was added in 1995.

Chaco Canyon Trading Post★★

Take CR 7800 (NR 45) west off US 550 at Nageezi Trading Post. At mile 11.4 the road junctions with NM 57; go left on NM 57 for six miles to a road barricade, then left for .4 mile to the site, which is on the left side.

Description: *Abandoned.* The original trading post was actually built onto the ancient Pueblo Bonito ruins. It was moved in 1923 a short distance to the west, close to Pueblo Del Arroyo. Both sites are within the Chaco Culture National Historical Park, and the remains have been completely removed and cleaned up. A later post was established by

Glen Whiteman in 1946 just outside the Park boundry. A cement slab and other ruins remain at this site.

History: Al Wetherill started the original post in 1897 and sold out to the Hyde Brothers (Hyde Exploring Expedition) in 1898. The Hydes hired Richard Wetherill as the trader and manager. He subsequently assumed ownership in 1902, and it was sold to the Miera family of Cuba, New Mexico around 1910, shortly after Wetherill's murder. In 1912, the owners of the post at the original site were Charles Spader and his partner, Edward Doonan, who was also shot and killed at the post during a robbery. They were followed by Elias Armijo in 1918 and Gus Griffin, who acquired it in 1923 and moved it to the Pueblo Del Arroyo site. He was followed by Wales Smith (1931), A. P. Springstead (1932), and Arthur Tanner (1937). Owners at the last location outside the Park were Glen Whiteman (1946), Leonard Taft (1952), Dee Stolworthy and Harry Batchelor (1954). The Navajo tribe took it over and closed it in 1973.

The original Chaco Canyon Trading Post, about 1900. Note the Pueblo Bonito ruins in background from which material was taken for the trading post. (Farmington Museum, #91.32.2)

The second Chaco Canyon Trading Post was built in 1923 by Gus Griffin. The photo shows Wade and Lorain Smith in the doorway. (Photo by George A. Grant. Courtesy of National Park Service, Chaco Culture National Historical Park, Negative #70446)

Beams for the roof of the original post were taken from the Pueblo Bonito ruins. The store was a small, one-story appendage to the ruins, about 15 x 20 feet. In his book *Anasazi*, Frank McNitt writes, "it was tight, snug and small and crowded with the dry goods, harness, galvanized ironware and rope, the boxed, bagged or canned food supplies, the axes, chains, lamps and fuel oil, and a few of the novel sundries and an assortment of candy which the Indians would want in bartering their wool and blankets or in pawning their jewelry."

A large rock wall called "Threatening Rock" was located just above the old Pueblo Bonito ruins. In January, 1941 it finally collapsed and fell on the ruins and site of the original post. Due to the tremendous volume of rock, it has never been excavated.

Escrito Trading Post★★
HCR 17, Box 1000, Cuba, NM 87013, (505) 568-4478

Located on US 550, approximately 48 miles south of Bloomfield, NM.

Description: *Renovated.* The post has been relocated, enlarged, and modified; but definitely not modernized. The store occupies a large building constructed of wood, cinder block, and metal siding (an architecture known as "trading post conglomerate") and has a rather old, well-used look. The owner still does some trading and sells groceries and other general merchandise needed by the local Navajo clientele. There is a small cafe located inside the store, which is somewhat unusual.

History: The original Escrito Trading Post, started in 1947 by Odie Chapman, was located in an old hogan on what eventually became the Bloomfield-Cuba highway right-of-way. Jim Mauzy leased it from around 1951 to 1955. In 1954, the highway department required the old hogan trading post to be moved. The post was relocated to the other side of the highway and about a quarter mile to the west. Odie Chapman resumed the store operation when Mauzy moved out and opened another store currently called Lybrook Mercantile about one mile futher south on Hwy. US 550. Odie's son Al Chapman took over operation of the Escrito store in 1965. Two years later it was destroyed by fire and was subsequently rebuilt a short distance away at its present location. In 1977, Al Chapman also assumed ownership of the Lybrook Mercantile store.

Original Escrito Trading Post started in an old hogan, about 1947. (Farmington Mueum, #89.17.44)

Counselor Trading Post★

P.O. Box 9766, Hwy. 550, Counselor, NM 87018, (505) 568-4453

Located on US 550, 54 miles south of Bloomfield, NM.

Description: *Renovated.* The post is still at its original site, but the building has been replaced. In 1968 a large metal building was built over the top of the original post, which was adobe and considerably smaller and incorporated within the new building.The post sells groceries and general merchandise and still does some trading, as well as functioning as a local post office.

History: Jim Counselor established the post in 1931. Subsequent owners were Leonard Taft (1945), Leonard Taft & Harold McDonald (1957), Harold and Jane McDonald (1967), and Jane McDonald (1988-2002). Harold McDonald, who was also a partner of Leonard Taft in the ownership of Blanco Trading Post, was killed at the Blanco post in 1988 by a young Navajo in a robbery.  After that, Counselor was owned by his wife Jane until her death in 2002. Her son Lewis, along with other members of the McDonald family, are the current owners. Jim Counselor was one of the earlier traders in the Largo Canyon area, which has never been officially part of the reservation. Prior to 1919, he worked for Doc Haynes at his trading post located about four miles north of Counselor. In the early years, the Counselor post was often used as field headquarters by archaeologists from the east who were studying old Navajo defensive sites located in the surrounding region. Jim and Ann Counselor wrote a book about Counselor trading days entitled *Wild, Wooly and Wonderful.*

Simpson Trading Post★★

Located on the east side of Gallegos Wash approximately
19 miles southeast of Farmington, NM. Follow NM 371
south of Farmington (intersection NM 371 & Murray
Dr.) for 6.4 miles to CR 7010. Turn east on CR 7010 for
7.7 miles then south on NR 4047 for 4.5 miles. Turn
west here onto a dirt road and go .7 mile to the site.

Description: *Abandoned.* All that remains are portions of the walls of the store and house and a small segment of the barn. The old post was originally an L-shaped adobe building, about 12 x 20 feet, with the  usual bullpen arrangement interior. In addition, there was a house and, across the road, a large barn and corrals. The dirt road on which the Simpson post was located was the main route between Farmington and Albuquerque by way of Chaco Canyon until the 1920s. It was replaced by what eventually became US 550. It was an off-reservation post located on private land in what is known as the "checkerboard" area (see Introduction).

History: The post was established in 1896 by Richard Thomas Flindell "Dick" Simpson, who had come from England just three years earlier. Before Simpson started the post, the site had been headquarters for the Carlisle Cattle Company, a rough outfit continually involved in range disputes with Navajos and any others who came on their unfenced land. Simpson did a large trade in fine Navajo rugs, and one of his best weavers was his wife, a Navajo named Yana-pah. She was one of the first to produce a Yei design in her rugs.

Simpson sold the post in 1927 to Progressive Mercantile Company, composed of the partners Al Foutz, Wilard Stolworthy, and Bert and Sheldon Dustin. The post was later bought out by Al Foutz and his son Russell. Shortly afterward, it was closed and moved about a mile north to Gallegos Wash and renamed the Gallegos Sheep & Mercantile Company, commonly known as the Gallegos Store. It was closed in 1972, and the site was cleared when the Navajo tribe began developing their irrigation project.

The Progressive Mercantile Company, formed a few years after 1903, was a general mercantile store and wholesale supply house for area trading posts. The company bought or built trading posts and would then install a young couple as manager and give them a ten percent interest in the store. The company would supply the merchandise for the store and handle the sale of the wool and livestock, getting a commitment from each store for what they would deliver. Eventually they controlled twenty-two trading posts, most of them in New Mexico. The Foutz family was the largest family of traders in the eastern part of the Navajo Reservation, followed by the Richardsons and Babbitts who worked the Arizona part.

Bisti Trading Post★★

Located directly across from the Methodist Mission on CR 7290, 3.4 miles east off NM 371; this junction is 29 miles south of Farmington, New Mexico

Description: *Abandoned.* The post burned in 1971. The ruins were bulldozed. No trace of it remains, an unfortunate loss as this was one of the more historic and authentic old posts around. The suspected cause of the fire was arson.

History: The early history of this post is uncertain, but it is believed that a man named Hunter (possibly Billy Hunter) may have established it around 1897. The post was subsequently sold to Joe Wynn and then to Walter Beck in 1924. Next, Walter Beck and Eli Cline became partners. Following the deaths of first Cline and then Beck, their wives assumed ownership, and Cline's son, Jack, operated the post and then took over ownership around 1930. Roy Burnham, the next owner, sold it to his son Bob and Roy Foutz around 1939. Bob Burnham assumed ownership in

Bisti Trading Post, about 1969. (Photo courtesy of Clayton Bond)

1946. Bob Burnham was followed by Karl Ashcroft, with his son Kay and Bill Palmer as partners in 1947; Karl and Kay Ashcroft in 1950; Kay and brother Lamar Ashcroft in 1955; Lamar Ashcroft and Theo Bond in 1958, and finally Clayton Bond in 1959 until it burned in 1971.

Clayton Bond behind the counter at Bisti Trading Post, 1969. (Photo courtesy of Clayton Bond)

The trading post site is located close to the nearly 4,000 acre Bisti Badlands Wilderness Area, established in 1984 and administered by the Bureau of Land Management. The area contains unique rock formations composed of unusually eroded sandstone pillars with slender spires capped with wider, harder stone on top. The formation is called "Bisti" by the Navajo, giving the Badlands and the trading post their name.

Original Bisti Trading Post, about 1920. (Photo courtesy of Jack Kline)

Getting a tow out of Chaco wash. (Photo courtesy of Jack Kline)

Tsaya Trading Post★★★

P. O. Box 298, Kirkland, NM 87417, (505) 786-7007

Located on a dirt road 1.5 miles east of NM 371, 49.3 miles south of Farmington, New Mexico. Turnoff is marked by a small sign saying "Savage's Trading Co."

Description: *Abandoned.* Only portions of the original walls remain. The area where the old post was located is quite scenic and unique, making a visit worthwhile. At the head of a small box canyon about 300 yards above the old post's ruins is a cool spring in a cave surrounded by boulders etched with names and dates, some as old as 1887.

Ruins of Tsaya Trading Post in 1997

History: The post was established by H. L. Haines in 1885. Haines abandoned the post in 1895, and it was reopened by Harvey Shawyer in 1906. He was followed by Albert and George Blake in 1910; Roy Burnham in 1918; Progressive Mercantile with Rual "Chunky" Tanner as a partner in 1927; and Karl Ashcroft and his son Kay in 1945. Following Karl's death in 1955, Kay took over the ownership. He closed the original post in 1961 and opened a more modern store the same year 2.4 miles farther south. The road on which the new store is located became NM State Hwy. 371 when it was completed in 1983. Kay Ashcroft is the current owner, and Ross, Kay's son, became a partner in 1986 and manages the store. On the hilltop overlooking the old ruins, a more recent, somewhat unusual store was built by George and Rena Savage in 1987 on land owned by Kay Ashcroft. Ashcroft still owns the old trading post site, so as not to compete with the new store, it does not sell groceries, but offers just about everything else.

Tsaya, short for Tsaya-chas-kesi meaning "water under the rock," is an off-reservation post located in the "checkerboard" area, thus accounting for its private ownership. In the early days of its existence it was one of the most remote trading posts, rarely visited by white men. Richard Wetherill, who explored and excavated the Mesa Verde and Chaco Canyon ruins, was shot and killed in a wash a few miles from the old Tsaya post. On the afternoon of June 22, 1910, a Navajo named Chischilly Begay came to Tsaya, purchased two boxes of cartridges from George Blake, rode up the wash toward Pueblo Bonito in Chaco Canyon, and killed Wetherill. The suspected motive was revenge for a beating given Begay's brother-in-law by Bill Finn, a cowboy who worked for Wetherill. More detail on Wetherill's life and murder can be found in the book *Anasazi* by Frank McNitt.

Torreon Trading Post*
P. O. Box 2259, Cuba, NM, 87013, (505) 731-2255

Located on NM 197, 27 miles west of Cuba, NM.

Description: *Converted.* The current store is a trading post in name only. It occupies a fairly large, white metal building with a small metal awning built across the front. The interior is a typical self-service grocery store with gas pumps out front. The store does not resemble a trading post either inside or outside, and no arts and crafts are available.

History: The original Torreon trading post was started in 1916, but by whom or precisely where is uncertain. In 1930, Gibb Graham built a new trading post building just east of where the present store is located. This post burned in the early 1950s following a tragic incident involving Graham's son Hooch. He was trying to collect some bills for his father and got into a fight with a local Navajo. Shots were fired by both sides, and Hooch was killed. Shortly after, the trading post was burned down. It was then rebuilt with cut stone at the same location for Gibb Graham by Jay Smith. Graham left the area after the incident, but continued to own the store and other property with Wallace Anderson as his manager. Maurice Tanner acquired it in 1964 and built the current store next door in 1969. The old post was then used as a residence and later as a laundromat. His son, Javen Tanner, operated the new store for a while. He sold it to Thriftway Corp. in 1989, which in turn sold out to Giant Industries in 1997. The current owner is Red Mesa Express, which bought the store in December, 2001.

Borrego Pass Trading Post★★★★
P. O. Box 329, Prewitt, NM, 87045, (505) 786-5396

Located on NR 48, 9.8 miles in from its junction with NM 371; then right .3 mile on gravel road.

Description: *Original.* The store has retained the trading post decor and atmosphere and is located in a beautiful, semi-remote setting. The original store, which was built from pinyon logs and adobe, has had additions built across the front and to the back and side for living quarters. It currently has a white stucco exterior and is very neat and well-kept. The interior of the store is clean and bright with shelves filled with boxed and canned goods. Besides groceries and gas, the store sells hats, clothes, hardware, and other general merchandise, and has a good collection of rugs and old artifacts. There is a large, old stone warehouse next to the store, and many trees are planted around the post, giving it a cool, attractive appearance.

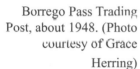

Borrego Pass Trading Post, about 1948. (Photo courtesy of Grace Herring)

History: The original post was built by Ben Harvey in the late '20s on land that he had homesteaded. He was heavily in debt to John Kirk and ended up turning the store over to him to relieve his indebtedness. Shortly after, Kirk hired Bill and Jean Cousins to run the store for him. Two years later, in 1937, the Cousins left when Kirk sold the post to Vernon Bloomfield. In 1939, Bloomfield was shot in the back by two teenage Navajo boys in a robbery attempt. No one else was around at the time, so Bloomfield drove himself to the hospital in Gallup. The boys were caught and sent away to boarding school as punishment. Bloomfield sold the post a year later to his brother-in-law, Don Smouse. After Smouse's death the family retained ownership of the post. Merle and Rosella Moore, who operated Mariano Lake Trading Post for twelve years, became the managers in 1991, and until 1999 did an outstanding job in maintaining the trading post atmosphere. The Moores were followed by Sonny Gonzales, the current manager of the store.

The post started with the store, wareroom, and residence in one building. After two or three years the large, sandstone warehouse (mentioned above), a large barn, and corrals were added. The area is called Debe be-atine in Navajo, meaning "sheep pass" — the pass over which Navajos would herd the sheep they had taken from Pueblos and

Mexicans. The Continental Divide passes through the area which, with its rolling countryside and red sandstone buttes and canyons, is one of the more scenic parts of the reservation.

Smith Lake Trading Post★
P. O. Box 90, Smith Lake, NM 87365, (505) 786-7307

Located on NM 371, 12 miles north of Thoreau, NM.

Description: *Converted.* The current store is in a blue metal building with bright paintings across the front. The interior of the store is similiar

to a small self-service grocery store and also houses the local post office. In addition to groceries, it carries videos, auto supplies, some general merchandise, and a small room with artifacts and a collection of Kachina dolls. It no longer functions as a trading post.

History: The original Smith Lake Trading Post, located about a half mile to the west of the current store, was started by L. C. Smith around 1906. Some of the earlier owners included Charlie McGee, followed by Al Tietjen who owned it in the 1940s. It was subsequently closed until the Foutz Trading Co. took it over in 1962. In 1981, Keith Foutz closed the old post and built the current store by the highway. Subsequent owners of the new store included Maurice Christenson and son Danny, followed by Roxanne Heath. Ted Gonzales, the current owner, bought it in 1993. The original post was in a fairly large, cut stone building with gas pumps out front. After closing, it remained in good condition until it burned down in 1995. The stone walls remained standing for a couple years and then were torn down and the stone carted off for use elsewhere. All that is left is a small amount of stone rubble showing the outline of the walls.

Pinedale Trading Post
P. O. Box 3127, Gallup, NM 87305, (505) 786-7767

> *Located on NR 11, 18.8 miles west of NM 371, then .3*
> *mile north on a graded dirt road. (NR 11 is designated*
> *NR 49 where it leaves NM 371.)*

Description: *Converted.* The store is housed in a large, plain white metal building. This replacement for the original Pinedale Trading Post no longer functions as a trading post.

History: The origin of the original post is not certain, but it is believed to have been started by Jimmy Brown around 1905. George and Dan Christensen acquired it in 1937 and sold it to Phil and Keith Foutz in 1953, with Keith taking over ownership in 1962. The original post burned around 1981. Foutz relocated it in a metal building about 1.2 miles northeast and operated it as a self-service convenience store. When Thriftway Corp. bought the store in 1992, they moved it across the road into an existing building that had been used as a laundromat. The other building was then torn down and hauled away. In 1996, Sunwest Stores took it over and then sold it to Henry and Ester King in 1998, who closed it in 2001. It was reopened in 2002 by Josie Gonzales.

Outlaw Trading Post★★
P. O. Box 328, Church Rock, NM 87311, (505) 863-1329

> *Located at the Red Rock State Park campground, which*
> *is just north of I-40, about 10 miles east of Gallup,*
> *NM.*

Description: *Renovated.* The building is made of cut stone, in good condition and very authentic looking. The interior retains the old trading post atmosphere, with wooden floors, shelves lining the walls with canned goods and other merchandise, and old counters forming the bullpen arrangement. It primarily sells groceries to the locals and campers. Adjacent to the trading post is a modern campground with water and electric hook-ups for RVs.

History: The original trading post, which was located about 100 yards east of the present store, was established by Charles Frederick in 1888. It was originally called Church Rock Ranch and Trading Post (there is an inscription etched on the large sandstone rock a short distance to the northeast of the current store). Harry Richards bought out the post in 1926, moved it to its present location, and renamed it Outlaw. Edward Vanderwagen leased it in 1940 for a couple years. Harry Richards' son, W. J. Richards, took it over in 1942 and sold it to the Intertribal Ceremonial Association in 1972. It eventually became part of the Red Rock State Park, which is operated by the City of Gallup under an agreement with the State of New Mexico.

Prewitt Trading Post★★

P. O. Box 553, Prewitt, NM 87045, (505) 876-4041

> **Located on old Hwy. 66, 10 miles east of Thoreau; take the Prewitt exit off I-40 and go east 1.5 miles to the store.**

Description: *Closed.* The current store is located about one-half mile east of the original Prewitt Trading Post. It is a rustic store with old vegas in the roof and a stucco exterior painted light tan. Additions were added to the rear in the 1950s. The interior still resembles an old-time store, and it carries groceries, auto supplies, and other general merchandise needed by the local population — both

Anglo and Native American. It also takes pawn, but does not cater to the tourist or carry any arts and crafts.

History: The first trading post in the area is reported to have been started in 1896. Robert Prewitt ran a post (most likely the same one) in 1916. Justin LaFont took it over around 1948 and closed it in 1958 when work began on the new Interstate Highway. The current store was started by Charlie Williams in 1945. It was basically a gas station, small grocery and curio store, and did not function as a trading post. Dave and Betty Ortega bought the store in 1950 and changed the operation so that it began functioning like a typical trading post. They also changed the name to Zuni Mountain Trading Post. After 1980 they began leasing it out to various parties including Ron Smith, Fred Dodson, Fred Elkins, and most recently Rufus and Marlene Thomas, who leased it in 1988, renamed it Prewitt Trading Post, and closed it in 2002.

OTHER ABANDONED TRADING POSTS

■ **Ojo Alamo:** It was located on Hunter Wash about twenty miles northwest of Chaco Culture National Historic Park. Established by Richard Wetherill for the Hyde Exploring Expedition in 1898, John Wetherill took it over in 1903 and closed it in 1906. The rubble of a stone foundation is all that remains.

■ **Otis: (Also called Tsah Tah Trading Post)** It was located three miles in on NM 57, which leaves US 550 at Blanco Trading Post. Started by a Mr. Otis in 1926, Red Bloomfield bought it in 1954. It closed in 1970. Nothing remains.

■ **Kimbeto: (Also called Kinnebito)** It is located on CR 7800, 8.5 miles in from its junction with US 550 at Nageezi Trading Post. It was established by Hyde Exploring Expedition in 1901, followed by

Percy Starr (1902), Sam Snyder (1905), a man named Hensley, Will Finn, and Richard Wetherill (1909), John Arrington (1915), C. "Shorty" Widdows (1916), George Christensen (1951), Dee Stolworthy (1952), Red Bloomfield (1955), and Harry Batchelor (1957) who closed it in 1973. The building is still standing but is in poor condition. The original post was located about one-half mile north, and only the remains of the foundation and tumbled sandstone walls remain.

■ **Escavada:** It was located on Escavada Wash, just off CR 7900, 8.7 miles south of its junction with US 550. It was established in 1891 by Hans Neumann and closed by Jim Brimhall in 1920. Nothing remains.

■ **Lybrook:** It was located on US 550, forty-nine miles south of Bloomfield, New Mexico. It was established by Will Lybrook in 1922, with the assistance of Jim Counselor, and ceased operating as a trading post in 1935 following Lybrook's death in an auto accident. It was a massive two-story stone building that served both as a residence and a trading post. After Lybrook's death it was used mainly as an inn to house local workers until it burned down in 1966. Some foundation stones remain.

■ **Doc Haynes:** It was located one-quarter mile east of CR 379, about five miles north of Counselor Trading Post. It was started by John "Doc" Haynes in 1901 and closed in 1930. Ruins from the building remain.

■ **Largo:** It was located on CR 379 about 12.5 miles from US 550, then .2 mi. east of the road. It was started by Jim Counselor about 1918 and closed a few years later. Rubble from the walls remains.

■ **La Posta: (Also called Cabezon)** It is located off Co. Rd. 39, 12.5 miles east of US 550; this junction is approximately twenty miles south of Cuba, New Mexico. The trading post was started at an unknown time by two men of German origin, Kisenbach and Haberland. It was sold to Dick Heller and John Pflueger in 1881, with Heller buying out Pflueger in 1894. At the time, the village of La Posta (later renamed Cabezon) consisted of nearly 150 families. It was a stop on the stage routes and wagon trails westward from Santa Fe. The store finally closed in 1947, and the families began moving away about a year later. The village eventually became deserted and took on ghost town status, with crumbling adobe buildings still present.

Ruins of Dick Heller's old trading post in ghost town of Cabezon, 2003.

■ **Tiz-na-tzin:** Its site not located. An approximate location is south of Coal Creek Wash, about halfway between Bisti and Tsaya, forty miles south of Farmington, New Mexico. It was started by "Old Man" Swires about 1878. Win Wetherill ran it for Hyde Exploring Expedition Co. in 1900, followed by Harvey Shawyer and Bert McJunkins. It was closed around 1920.

■ **Joe Tanner:** Turn off NM 371 about 52 miles south of Farmington, New Mexico onto CR 7760; go 3.2 miles and turn left onto a dirt road for 1.6 miles to the site. It was established by Joe Tanner around 1930. After Tanner's death in 1944, Chee Dodge took it over, ran it as a ranch and then sold out to Glen Williams, followed by Kay Ashcroft in 1958, and the Navajo tribe in 1964, which then closed it. Stone buildings remain. The barn and corral appear to still be in use.

■ **White Rock:** It is located on CR 7760, 4.8 miles west of its junction with NM 371. It was established by Willis Martin around 1905, followed by James Gibson in early 1920s, James' brother, Walter "Bud" Gibson, (1939), Karl Ashcroft (1941), Karl Ashcroft and Bill Palmer (1945), Kay and Lamar Ashcroft (1952), and Kay Ashcroft (1957). It closed in 1961 and was later sold to the Navajo tribe. The stone buildings remain.

■ **Crownpoint:** It was located about two miles southwest of Crownpoint, New Mexico. Established in 1911 by Jim Matchin, subsequent owners are unknown until John and Evelyn Simms took it over. Don Walker bought it in 1947 and changed the name from Simms Store to Crownpoint Trading Co. He was followed by Willard Palmer in 1972, Phil Foutz in 1985, then the post burned down two years later.

■ **Mariano Lake:** The post is located on NR 49, eleven miles west of NM 371. It is believed to have been started by Charlie Weidemeyer around 1890. Later owners included Dee Westbrook, E. W. Zimmerman (1936), Dan Christensen (1943), Charles Ashcroft (1953), Norman Ashcroft (1957), Keith, Phil and Cal Foutz (1967), and Merle and Rosella Moore (1978). The last owners, Charles and Marie Westmoreland, took it over in 1990 and closed it in 1993. The store was located on the old stage road to Gallup and once served as a stagecoach stop. The building is still in good condition.

■ **Seven Lakes:** Its site not located. An approximate location is on NR 9, about fourteen miles east of NM 371. It is believed to have been started by George McAdams about 1896 and closed in the 1940s.

■ **Whitehorse:** It was located just south of NR 9, twenty-four miles east of NM 371. It was started by Pauline Buck about 1920, followed by Pratt Nelson in the late 1940s, Bill Palmer (1955), Maurice Tanner (1959), George Huntsman (1963), Buddy Spicer (1964), and Thriftway Corp. (1978). Al Grieve leased it from Thriftway from 1984 to 1990 and then closed it. It was torn down within a year or two and nothing remains.

■ **Pueblo Alto:** It is located on NR 9, forty-two miles east of NM 371. The original trading post, located about four miles north of Pueblo Pintado, was built by Ralph Tucker in 1915 and was known as **Tucker's Store**. In 1918 a tragic incident occurred there when Tucker got into a disagreement with a couple of local Navajos who had been drinking. The store was later burned down. Eighteen-year-old Pat Smith, the youngest of four Indian trader brothers, was watching the store for Tucker while he went to Albuquerque. The Indians came to the store after it closed and talked him into letting them in. He was subsequently killed and left in the store while it burned. Tucker rebuilt the store but died shortly thereafter. It was then sold by his widow to Ed Sargent and Bob Smith (Pat Smith's older brother) with Lester Setzer as manager. Arthur Tanner bought it in 1939 and moved it in 1940 to a location about a mile and a half north of the present site. It was moved again to its current location in 1984 by Maurice Tanner, Arthur's son. He sold it to Thriftway Corp. in 1990, followed by Giant Industries in 1997, and Red Mesa Express in December, 2001, which then converted it to a laundromat. They have since sold it to the current owner, Dennis Buckman, who also owns the Pueblo Pintado store.

■ **Star Lake:** It was located six miles east of Pueblo Alto and two miles north of NR 9. It was started by Albert Starr in 1898 and sold to George Blake in 1913; others included Richard Frankel in 1917, Pauline Buck, Bob Smith, Hendrix Cox, and Maurice Tanner in 1961. It was closed by Tanner in 1963. Some rubble remains.

■ **Tinian:** It is located four miles northwest of Torreon. It was started by Arthur Tanner in 1946, it burned in 1950, and Hendrix Cox ran it during the '50s out of a hay barn. Maurice Tanner took it over in 1961, rebuilt the old store, and then closed it for good in 1970. Nothing remains.

■ **Ojo Encino:** It was located on NR 474, eighteen miles northwest of NM 197. This junction is sixteen miles west of Cuba, New Mexico. The trading post is no longer in operation and has been converted into a residence. It was started by Ralph Duran around 1966 and was last operated by Ralph Duran, Jr.. An earlier trading post, the predecessor to the last store, was located at the base of the hill below the more recent site. It was started by Bob Smith in the early 1900s and closed around 1930.

■ **Standing Rock:** It was located fifteen miles west of Crownpoint on NR 9, north of the highway .4 miles. The original trading post, established in 1921, was located just behind the more recent store. Floyd Burnham took it over in 1933. Al Grieve leased it in 1973 and closed it in 1977. It burned down two years later, followed shortly by the barn. Nothing is left of the old post. There had not been a store in the area until 1988 when Rosalie Plummer started the Standing Rock Mini Mart, which she closed in 1991.

■ **Shillingburg: (Also called Biggs Store)** It was located on NR 11 (Dalton Pass Road) about two miles southwest of NR 9. It was started in 1906, by a party unknown. John Kirk and Don Shillingburg became the owners in 1919, with Shillingburg taking it over in 1920, followed by Hendrix Cox and Kleo and Horace Biggs (1946), and Bill Palmer (1957). It closed in 1959. Nothing remains.

■ **Springstead:** It is located about five miles northeast of Outlaw Trading Post. It was started by A. P. Springstead in the late 1930s and operated by him and his son until it closed in 1985. Old building remains.

Old Shillingburg Trading Post (also known as Biggs Store), about 1930's. (Photo courtesy of Don Shillingburg)

■ **Fort Wingate:** It was located on NM 400, three miles south of I-40, at the community of Fort Wingate. It was started by Howard Wilson in 1925, followed by A. L. Williams (1935), Dick White (1940), and Paul Merrill (1946). It closed about 1960. Prior to this trading post, a store existed at the old military fort. Willi Spiegelberg was the first civilian trader there in 1868, followed by John Waters (1869), Henry Reed (1872), Lambert Hopkins (1890), and James May (ca.1900).

■ **Perea:** It was located about thirteen miles east of Gallup on old Hwy. 66. It was started by George Christensen in 1935, sold to Jewell McGee in 1942, followed by a Mr. McCarty. McCarty sold it to the Foutz Trading Co. in 1954. They closed it in 1956.

■ **Guam:** It was located twenty-two miles east of Gallup, north of I-40 and the railroad tracks. It was started by Hans Neumann in 1899, followed by Horabin & McGaffey in 1913, and closed around 1915. A fire destroyed the building around 1955. Nothing remains.

■ **Staples:** It was located one mile west of Guam. It was started in 1926 by Berton Staples. The post was housed in a large Spanish-style building and became a popular visiting place for artists, writers, and Hollywood actors. It was later sold to Charlie Newcomb in 1939 and burned down in 1955. Nothing remains.

■ **Red Arrow, Thoreau Mercantile, Lewis:** All were located in the Thoreau area. **Red Arrow** existed from 1896 to 1941. Owners included Gallup Merchantile, Evelyn Simms, and Jimmy Matchin, and Ronald Carlene in the mid-1930s. It closed in 1941. **Thoreau Mercantile**, also known as **Jones Mercantile**, existed from 1896 to 1970; Homer Jones owned it from 1921 until 1951, when he sold it to Dan Rangel. **Lewis**

Trading Post is reported to have started around 1946 and closed in the 1970s; nothing else is known about it.

■ **Hyde Exploring Expedition Store:** It was located in the Thoreau area, and was started by Hyde Brothers in 1898 and closed around 1910. Nothing remains.

■ **Horabib & McGaffey:** It was located in the Thoreau area and was started by Al Wetherill and W. S. Horabib around 1900. Later McGaffey replaced Wetherill; the post closed about 1913. Nothing remains.

Chapter 4

Shiprock

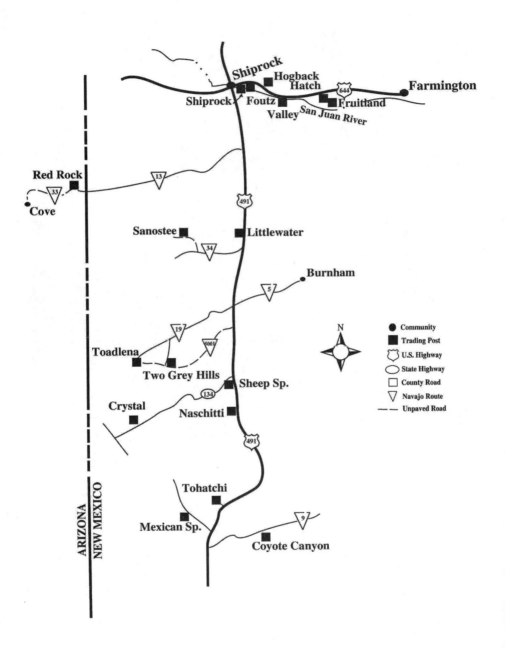

Fruitland Trading Company★★
P. O. Box 328, Fruitland, NM 87416, (505) 598-1528

On US 64 go 8.4 miles west of Farmington; turn south onto CR 6675 for .9 mile to stoplight; make a slight jog to the left to CR 6677; trading post located on right side.

Description: *Closed.* The post is still at its original location, where it had been in continuous operation until its recent closing in 1999. The current owner has an office housed in the building. The closing was unfortunate as it was a historic old post and one of the more authentic ones still in existence, with the porch out front, old concrete floors, and wooden counters. The moving of the  Post Office, which was located across the road and attracted the local population to the area, was the major factor affecting its closing. This is somewhat ironic, since the trading post was probably the reason the Post Office originally located where it was. Nothing much has changed to the exterior appearance of the trading post since it closed.

History: The post was established by Hambleton B. Noel in 1886. Subsequent owners were Eli Cline (1908), Eli Cline and Walter Beck (1926), Eli's son, Jack Cline (1935), Mrs. Jack Cline, Gary and Jack Cline, Jr. (1955), Jack Cline, Jr. (1966), Jim Murphy and Bob Jacobson (1971), Barbara Busey (1977), Ernest Soloman (1995), and Leon Smalley (1996-present). The main portion of the current building was built in 1925. The small square section to the left was part of the original post, which was located just behind and adjacent to this section. It was used as a residence by the owner in more recent years. Navajos referred to the post as "Burnt Bread Trading Post." Before moving to Fruitland, Eli Cline had a bakery in Farmington which burned, and the Navajos (who have a great sense of humor) called him "Burnt Bread" and his son, "Little Bread."

Old Fruitland Trading Company store, about 1929

Hatch Bros. Trading Post★★★★
36 Riverside Dr., Fruitland, NM 87416, (505) 598-6226

Located on CR 6677, .4 mile on down the road past Fruitland Trading Company store.

Description: *Original.* Stewart and Claude Hatch started the post in 1949 and are still the current owners. The post is of fairly recent origin, but it closely resembles old-time posts. The building is of cement block construction, in good condition, and fairly authentic looking as opposed to some of the more modern convenience stores that many of the old posts have been converted into. It has a beautiful location next to a lake with large cottonwoods all around. There are a number of outbuildings and a corral adjacent to the store. The interior appearance and the way the store is operated have changed little since the post was established. It has the old "bullpen" arrangement with shelves behind the counters filled with neatly stacked canned goods and other merchandise, and it is one of the more authentic and quaint posts on or around the reservation.

In addition to the usual groceries, the post carries many items used by the Navajos that are not found in most convenience stores. It also has an excellent selection of Navajo rugs, primarily from the Two Grey Hills area.

History: Two old wagon roads used to meet just outside the post. Each came from a ford on the San Juan River, and were used until a bridge

Stewart Hatch at counter inside trading post, 1998.

was built nearby in the early '50s. The roads were the main access to the post and saw much wagon and horseback traffic. Even after the bridge was built, Stewart reported seeing an occasional wagon as late as 1968. Neither road is in existence today. A feature article written about the post appeared in Denver, Dallas, and Boston newpapers.

Valley Trading Company★★

P. O. Box 230, Waterflow, NM 87421, (505) 598-5133

Located on US 64, 11.7 miles east of Shiprock, NM.

Description: *Renovated.* The current store is still at the original site and is a very interesting place to visit. With its wooden floors and quaint interior, it is the closest thing to an old-time general store that

you will find around. It sells everything from gas, groceries, and meats to hay, hardware, vet and auto supplies, clothes, and anything else a rural resident might need. The clientele is predominantly Navajo, and a friendly atmosphere prevails between the store personnel and their customers.

History: Leo Warren started the store in 1931. He was followed by Ivan Marteneau, who sold it to Walter Ealum around 1952. Raymond Bradshaw became the owner in 1957, and his son Dean became a half partner in 1960. Dean took over full ownership in 1972 and is the current operator. The original store, which was made of adobe with a flat, dirt roof, has been enlarged and improved. Major renovation took place in 1977 when a new gabled roof was installed, a large wareroom was added on the side, and a residence was built onto the back. All additions were made of adobe blocks. Some were obtained from old buildings in the area, and others were made new at the location. Timbers for the roof were hauled in from the mountains and milled on the site.

Old Valley Trading Post, 1957. (Photo courtesy of Raymond Bradshaw)

Hogback Trading Company★★★
Waterflow, NM 87421, (505) 598-6606

Located on CR 6950 just north of US 64 (can be seen from highway), 8.6 miles east of Shiprock, NM.

Description: *Abandoned.* The last active trading post at the spot closed in 1969, and has sat vacant since then, gradually deteriorating. The building,

Lloyd Wheeler in front of old Hogback Trading Company, 1998.

Hogback Trading Post at the base of Hogback Ridge where Hank Hull rebuilt it, about 1895. (Farmington Museum, #87.12.20)

which is in poor condition, is made of adobe and stone with a stucco overlay and cement block additions. It was enlarged around 1910 and the exterior was last renovated in 1935, with interior remodeling in 1950.

History: The post was started in 1871 by Hank Hull and Tom White. This date is based on an old board from Hull's original trading counter with the date September 19, 1871 painted on it. Harry Baldwin, Hull's nephew, became the next owner from around 1900 until 1916, when Wilfred Wheeler bought it. Wheeler leased it to Joe Tanner and Willard Stolworthy from 1917 to 1918, and resumed operation until his son Lloyd took it over in 1950. Lloyd closed it in 1969 and built a new convenience store a short distance away on the improved Highway US 550 (currently US 64). Operation of that store was taken over in 1973 by his son Tom. The convenience store was sold in 1985, and an exceptional Indian arts and crafts store was built next door. It is currently operated by Tom Wheeler.

Hank Hull's original post, which was located closer to the San Juan River, was the site of a near Indian uprising in 1894, when a man named Welch, who worked for Hull, was shot by a Navajo after a quarrel. Following the arrival of a company of cavalry troops from Fort Wingate, the man who killed Welch, a Navajo called "Fat" was persuaded to surrender and was taken under arrest to Fort Wingate and subsequently tried and sentenced to federal prison at Fort Levenworth. Following this incident, Hull closed his first post, which was subject to flooding from the San Juan River, and moved it to the current location.

Foutz Trading Company★★
P. O. Box 1894, Shiprock, NM 87420, (505) 368-5790

Located on US 64, .7 mile east of the US 64/US 491 junction in Shiprock, NM.

Description: *Converted.* Both the interior and exterior of the building have been remodeled. However, the interior retains some of the old store atmosphere with the original wood floor and other furnishings still present. The store no longer functions as a trading post, but as an Indian arts and crafts store — selling supplies to local Navajos and buying their rugs, pottery, and other finished products for resale. The store is noted for its fine rugs and sandpaintings, and the Shiprock-Red Rock area is known for the colorful, high quality Yei and Yeibechai rugs produced there.

History: In 1909, Bruce Bernard acquired the old Shiprock Trading Post owned by Robert Baker, which was located at the foot of the hill just west of the current Foutz Trading Company store. In 1917, Bernard closed the old Shiprock post and constructed the building in which the Foutz store is currently located. His new business became known as Bruce Bernard General Merchandise. Bernard owned it until his death in 1952, after which the family retained ownership. Luther Manning operated the store for Bernard and the family from about 1928 until 1976, when Bruce Bernard III took over the operation. He closed the post in 1978, and it reverted to the Navajo tribe. Bill Foutz, the current owner, assumed the lease in 1982 and reopened the store, renaming it Foutz Trading Company.

Shiprock Trading Company★★
P. O. Box 906, Shiprock, NM 87420, (505) 368-4585

> *Located on US 64, at east edge of Shiprock, NM. .5 mile east of the US 64/US 491 junction.*

Description: *Converted.* The current building is of masonry construction painted light tan with rustic wood trim. It has been much enlarged and modernized and has recently undergone additional renovation. The arts and crafts section is separated by a partition from what used to be the grocery and general merchandise store. That part is currently used as

Old Shiprock Trading Post, about 1937. (Photo courtesy of Jed Foutz)

a combination pizza cafe and convenience store. The arts and crafts section has a good rug room and sells quality arts and crafts as well as the supplies needed to produce them.

History: This post, not to be confused with the original Shiprock Trading Post, was started by Matt Hubbard in 1894 and sold to Will Evans in 1917. It was originally located a short distance southeast of its present location and was relocated by Evans around 1924 when a new road was built, which eventually became the present US 64. Evans sold the store to the Jack Brothers (Vernon, Sylvan, Nelson, and Clarence) in 1948. Russell Foutz acquired the post in 1954 and turned it over to his nephew Ed Foutz in 1972, followed by Ed's son Jed Foutz in 1992, who operates it today as the Shiprock Trading Company.

Evans, who had artistic talent, painted geometric designs and ceremonial figures on the exterior of the trading post and also did paintings on the Hogback and Mancos Creek Trading Posts. Shortly after taking over the post, Evans assisted in the commerical development of the Yei blanket or rug, for which the area is still known. Less common than the Yei is the rug known as a Yeibechai, which also originated in the Shiprock-Red Rock area. It is similiar to the Yei, but depicts a line of Navajo dancers in profile, impersonating Yei figures and it usually has a border. Both rugs are of small size, usually less than 3 x 5 feet.

INDIAN TRADERS and government officials posed for this photograph at the Shiprock Fair in 1912. Bottom row, from left, unidentified government employee, Arthur Newcomb, Supt. Wm. T. Shelton, Joe Tanner, Louisa Wade Wetherill, John Wetherill. Second row: "Old Man" Hawley, Frank Mapel, Mrs. Edith Mapel, Crownpoint agent Samuel E. Stacher, George Bloomfield, Mrs. Ed. Davies, Ed Davies, Mary Davies, Third row: Herbert Redshaw, Al Foutz, Olin C. Walker, Will Evans, John Hunt, (last two unidentified). Top row: Sheldon Dustin, John Walker, Jess Foutz, Ike Goldsmith, Bert Dustin, Frank Noel, Fonnie Nelson, June Foutz, Bruce Bernard, unidentified government employee.

Red Rock Trading Post★★★

P. O. Box 100, Red Valley, AZ 86544, (928) 653-4555

Located on NR 13, 21.7 miles west of US 491; the NR 13/ US 491 junction is 7.2 miles south of Shiprock, NM.

Description: *Renovated.* Both the interior and exterior of the store have been remodeled and modernized, but it still retains some of the old

trading post appearance. The building is nearly 100 feet in length. A front porch made of wood with pole supports has been added, making it quite rustic and attractive. It is mainly a grocery store and also sells various hardware, yarn, and other craft items. It does limited trading, mainly for rugs, jewelry, wool, and sheep. The original building is incorporated into the rear of the present store. Part of the old building resembles a "vault" which is entered through a large steel door and contains Indian arts and crafts and other interesting artifacts. You may need to ask the current manager to show it to you. Behind the trading post is an interesting

Jewell McGee (center) in front of Red Rock Trading Post, about 1940. (Photo courtesy of Grace Herring)

old barn built around 1920 and a corral where sheep are kept. The area around the post is quite attractive with beautiful red rock formations, and the road past the store continues on a very scenic route through the Lukachukai Mountains over Buffalo Pass to NR 12.

History: The post was established by Olin C. Walker in 1907. In the first three years he had two partners, Mr. Whitcroft and then Matt Hubbard. Subsequent owners were Willis Martin (1918), Dutch Taft (1923), Corlis Stolworthy (1925) with Stokes Carson as a partner from 1926 to 1928, Corlis Stolworthy and Jewel McGee (1933), Jewel McGee (1942), Jewel McGee and Troy Kennedy (1948), Troy Kennedy (1966), Jed Foutz (1992-2003), and the current owner Red Rock Retailers, who acquired it in December, 2003. The original store was 20 x 40 feet with adjacent warerooms on each end. It had eighteen inch adobe and stone walls with large vegas (support beams) across the ceiling. Two subsequent additions were made across the front length of the store. The first was done when Taft owned it, and the second, now the front part of the present store and made of cement blocks, was done when McGee and Kennedy had it. The destinctive Yei blanket and the less common Yeibechai rug came from this area. Also, the sandpainting rug originated at this post.

Original Red Rock Trading Post, about 1910. (Photo courtesy of Jewell McGee)

Red Rock Trading Post interior, about 1910. (Farmington Museum, #1989.17.55)

Little Water Trading Post

HCR 4, P. O. Box 400, Shiprock, NM 87420, (505) 696-3242

Located on US 491, 22.5 miles south of Shiprock, NM.

Description: *Renovated.* The store closed recently, but will probably re-open in the near future. The store is of cinder block construction, painted white with red and blue trim, and was operated as a small self-service convenience store.

History: The original trading post at this location was a small, square log building started by Joe Wilkins around 1896 or '97. Because of bitter cold, windy conditions there, it was abandoned and moved to a more sheltered location in Sanostee Wash where he built the Sanostee Trading Post. The old Little Water site lay dormant for several years until Robert & Katherine Fulton reestablished the post in 1947 and made improvements. Partners Nelson Jack and Willard Leighton became owners of the post in 1955. Shortly afterward the store was enlatged with cement block additions, remodeled to its present condition and ceased functioning as a trading post. Following Willard's death in 1959, his widow, Marie Leighton, along with Derald Stock, assumed ownership until 1961, followed by Phil Foutz (1962), R. B. Foutz, Jr. (1974), Wilbur Martin (1983), Bill Pilgrim (1992), Cora Johnson (1996), Presley and Wesley Davis (2004), and Red Mesa Express as of June, 2006.

Sanostee Trading Post★★

> *Follow US 491 23.7 miles south of Shiprock; turn west*
> *onto NR 34 for 6.5 miles, then turn right on a graded*
> *dirt road for .6 mile.*

Description: *Closed.* The original post was a small stone and adobe building and included log sheds, a plank barn, and a string of corrals.

In 1986 a fire damaged portions of the old store, after which an addition made of tan colored, rough-face cement blocks was built onto the front. In recent years it functioned mainly as a convenience store selling gas, groceries, and other general merchandise, and operated the local post office. Although the store no longer functions as a trading post, its clientele are exclusively Navajo, and it still retains some of the trading post atmosphere. It has a somewhat remote setting. Located down in a wide arroyo cut by Sanostee Wash, it sits lower than the surrounding desert plateau.

History: Joe Wilkin, in partnership with Will Evans and Edwin Dustin, started the post in 1898. Will Evans & Frank Noel bought it in 1905 and sold out to Progressive Mercantile, followed by Jess Foutz and John Walker, Hugh Foutz, Hugh's son Munro Foutz, Thriftway Corp., and Navajo Nation Shopping Center, who closed it in June 1999. Robert Johnson re-opened it in April, 2005 and closed it in Sept., 2006.

In 1913, the Sanostee Trading Post was the mediation site for settling the Beautiful Mountain Uprising, which resulted from an attempt to enforce a law prohibiting plural marriages among the Navajo. In a camp above the Sanostee store, near the summit of the mountain, a small band of Navajos went into hiding. They were led by medicine man Bizhoshi, father of Little Singer, who had three wives. For more than two months they defied all efforts by the U. S. Government to dislodge them. It was the last time the United States used a large force of troops against Native Americans. All the Navajos eventually surrendered without bloodshed and were taken to Gallup and then on to Santa Fe to stand trial.

Toadlena Trading Post★★★★
P. O. Box 8014, Newcomb, NM 87455, (505) 789-3267

Turn west off US 491 at the Thriftway store, 31.8 miles south of Shiprock onto NR 19 and go 12.3 miles to end of pavement; then .4 mile on NR 5001 to the post.

Description: *Original.* The post has been closed at various times in the past, most recently in 1993. It was reopened for business by Mark Winter,

who has restored the interior in a manner that maintains the historic atmosphere of the old post. Shelves loaded with canned goods and other merchandise line the walls, old counters have been arranged to form the bullpen, and artifacts and various items hang from the ceiling. In addition to operating the post to serve area residents and visitors, Mr. Winter has created a weaving museum in honor of the weavers of the region. The Two Grey Hills weaving collection that forms the basis of the museum exhibits has been in the making for more than ten years under Winter's direction. It is one of the finest collections ever assembled — containing numerous documented examples from throughout the 20th century.

History: Merritt and Bob Smith started the post in 1909. Subsequent owners were George Bloomfield (1911), Charles and Grace Herring, Bloomfield's daughter and son-in-law (1936), Fred Carson (1956), and R. B. Foutz, Jr. (1958). It was closed from 1993 until 1997 when the current owner, Mark Winter, took it over.

The Navajo name for the post was "Toh-ha-lene," meaning "water bubbling up," which was corrupted by Anglos to Toadlena. The original post built by the Smiths was a small adobe building, measuring 18 x 37 feet. In 1927, George Bloomfield enlarged the original building by making additions on each end and at the rear, and covering the entire building with cut stone. It is still in good condition. The post is located in an attractive area close to the Chuska Mountains. It sits on a small hill overlooking the road to the Two Grey Hills Post, located 5.3 miles to the west. During the Bloomfield and Herring era the building and

Toadlena Trading Post, about 1925, before the gable roof and additions were added. (Photo courtesy of Grace Herring)

grounds around it were very well maintained, and it was one of the most attractive posts on the reservation. Bloomfield, along with Ed Davies of the Two Grey Hills Post, helped improve the quality of local weavers and were very instrumental in the development of the Two Grey Hills rug, which emerged about 1925.

George Bloomfield standing with friends outside his Toadlena Trading Post, about 1930. (Photo courtesy of Grace Herring)

Two Grey Hills Trading Post★★★★
Tohatchi, NM 87325, (505) 789-3270

Turn west off US 491 at the Thriftway store, 31.8 miles south of Shiprock, onto NR 19; go 7.3 miles, turn left onto NR 5000 for 3.1 miles, then turn left to the trading post.

Description: *Original.* This is one of the last remaining old style trading posts on the Navajo reservation and is one of the few that has not been converted into one of the convenience stores that are now so prevalent. It is one of a dying breed of about a dozen authentic trading posts scattered across the reservation. It is still located in the original building, which is made of cut stone with a tin roof. Two cement block additions, one on the left and one at the rear, blend very well with the original construction. In addition to a large selection of rugs, the post sells groceries and dry goods and does occasional trading.

History: The post was established by Joe Wilkin and Henry & Frank Noel in 1897. Subsequent owners included Henry & Frank Noel (1898), Henry & Hambleton Noel (1900), Win Wetherill (1902), Joe Reitz (1904), Joe Reitz & Ed Davies (1909), Ed Davies (1912), Willis Martin (1924), Morris Kirkpatrick (1930), Vic Walker (1936) with Walter Scribner as a partner in 1941, Willard & Marie Leighton (1948) with Nelson Jack as a partner from 1954 to 1958. Following Willard's death in 1959, his widow retained ownership for about a year and then sold one-half interest to the manager,

Les Wilson and weaver Shirley Brown, showing her Two Grey Hills rug.

Derald Stock. Stock subsequently sold his interest to Jack Powell in 1961. Two years later Derald Stock and Marie Leighton formed a partnership and took back the ownership from Powell. Following Stock's death in 1980, his widow Pat assumed her late husband's partnership with Marie Leighton. In 1983, Pat sold out to Marie, who then sold the post in 1986 to Les Wilson, the present owner.

From the area around this post originates the famous Two Grey Hills rug. It is believed the style for the rug began about 1915 and fully developed by 1925. Two early traders, Ed Davies at Two Grey Hills and George Bloomfield at Toadlena Post, were largely responsible for the development of this beautiful rug through endless hours spent instructing Navajo weavers in the region. The rugs have a geometric diamond pattern surrounded by a black border and, except for the border, are colored entirely with undyed shades of brown wool. It is uncertain how the name of the post originated, but one possible version is that it was named for two rocky, clay-covered hills or small mesas a little south of the post (although grey is not the dominant color). The post has been named to the New Mexico Register of Cultural Properties.

Sheep Springs Trading Post
P. O. Box 1454, Sheep Springs, NM 87364, (505) 732-4211

Located on US 491, 45.5 miles south of Shiprock, NM.

Desctiption: *Converted.* The trading post has been converted into a gas

and grocery convenience store. The old building, which was located next door to the current store, was torn down in the fall of 2003. It was made of adobe with a white stucco overlay, was in relatively good condition, and had more of the old trading post appearance than the smaller cinder-block building that replaced it.

History: The original post, which was located about one-half mile west, was started by Charles Newcomb in 1912 and was moved to its last location by Faun Taylor. Owners after Newcomb included Karl Ashcroft and Tom Dustin (1922), Tom Dustin (1925), Faun Taylor (1929), R. B. Foutz (1932), Lynn Helquest (1955), Raymond Carson (1969), Thriftway Corp. (1979), Carl and Leonard Todacheene (1982), and the current owner Red Mesa Express in 2001. The building in which the store is currently located was built by Lynn Helquest and was originally used as a cafe. When Carson acquired the post he moved it into the newer cinder block cafe building and used the old trading post building to house a laundromat which has since closed. The old building was also used as a post office until it was replaced by a metal structure built on the side of the current store.

The area where the post is located used to be a popular campsite for the military in the 1800s. A council with Narbona and other Navajo leaders was held there in 1847. The site was also used by troops on their way to the 1913 Beautiful Mountain Uprising.

Crystal Trading Post★★★

Take US 491 south from Shiprock for 45.5 miles; turn
west (at Sheep Springs TP) and follow NM 134 across
Washington Pass for 17.5 miles; turn right at the Crystal
sign and go .1 mile on pavement then take a sharp turn
left onto a dirt road for .4 mile to the site.

Description: *Closed.* The post has been closed since 1994 and probably
will not reopen. This is unfortunate as it was one of the few original, old-
time posts left. The original post was built out of logs hauled in from the
nearby mountains. At some later date it was remodeled and enlarged. Stone

walls were added, the
old log walls were
covered with stucco,
a metal addition was
added to the rear,
and the roof was
replaced with tin.
Even with these
changes the exte-
rior retains much of
its original, rustic appearance. The interior had some remodeling, but was
still relatively original until it closed. Since then, many of the interior furnishings have been removed or vandalized.

History: Joe Wilkin and Elmer Whitehorse started the post in 1894.
Subsequent owners were Joe Reitz and J. B. Moore (1896), J. B.
Moore (1897), Jesse Molohon (1911), C. C. Manning (1919), Charlie
Newcomb (1922), Jim Collyer and Faun Taylor (1936), H. M. Brimhall
(1944), Don Jensen (1946), Wade Townsend and Richard Mike (1981),
W. C. "Charley" Andrews (1986), Kit Hamilton (1990), and Bill Pilgrim
(1992-1994).

Crystal is located eight miles west of Washington Pass, named for
Colonel John M. Washington, who led troops over the pass in 1849.
The pass has since been renamed Narbona Pass by the Navajo Nation
in honor of the Navajo leader who was killed there by troops under

Colonel Washington. The pass area is heavily forested with pine and fir and is one of the most scenic parts of the reservation. As early as 1878 traders operated from tents during the summer in the area around Narbona Pass, but they probably did not maintain a year-round business due to the remoteness and heavy snows. These early traders included Romulo Martinez, the first known trader in the area, who started in 1878 and remained until 1881; Ben Hyatt from 1882 until 1884; Stephen Aldrich and Elias Clark in 1884; Elias Clark and Charles Hubble in 1884; Walter Fales in 1885; Michael Donovan in 1886, followed by Perry Williams in 1887.

Prior to when J. B. Moore took over the post, it had been run out of a tent. Moore built a permanent log structure and named it Crystal after a clear mountain spring that was located nearby. He sold it and left the area in 1911 as the result of a financial scandal for which he was not personally responsible. Moore contributed greatly to improving the quality of Navajo weaving. The early Crystal rug that Moore helped develop used bright red aniline dyes and bordered patterns and was strikingly different from the Crystal rugs of today. These rugs are woven with soft pastels and earth tone colors made from vegetable dyes. The Crystal rug is now considered one of the three most popular rug patterns.

Naschitti Trading Post*
HCR 330, Tohatchi, NM 87335, (505) 732-4208

***Located on US 491, 51 miles south of Shiprock and
west of the highway about 200 yards.***

Description: *Renovated.* The present store is housed in a fairly large

cement block building with a somewhat plain exterior painted white with red trim. The interior appearance is similiar to a typical small self-service grocery store. In addition to groceries, the post sells gas and general merchandise needed by the local Navajos. Like many of the old posts, however, it would be considered more a modern grocery store than an old-time trading post.

History: Thomas Bryan and his brother-in-law, Charlie Virden, established the post in 1881. C. C. Manning took it over in 1902 with Charlie Newcomb actually running the store as his manager. Manning sold it to Marshall Drolet around 1932. Drolet was followed by Fred Carson in 1951 and Decker Foutz in 1964. Red Mesa Express assumed ownership in 2001 and is the present owner.

The original post, which was located just behind the present one, had a large, attractive house adjoining it. The store and house burned to the ground around 1954, and only a stone fireplace that was part of an outside patio remains. According to Fred "Allen" Carson, Fred Carson's son, they immediately rebuilt the post at its present location, working practically around the clock in order to get it back in operation. The old post was one of the first to locate on the eastern slopes of the Chuska Mountains. Cavalry troops from Fort Robinson camped at the post during the 1913 Beautiful Mountain Uprising. The area around the post was a major livestock producing area with one of the largest annual cattle auctions on the reservation.

Tohatchi Trading Post

Located about .7 mile west of highway US 491, 23 miles north of Gallup, NM.

Description: *Closed.* This old trading post closed about twenty years ago, but could reopen someday. The present building was originally the warehouse for the trading post, which was located next to it. It was rebuilt and converted into the trading post itself when Walter and Troy Kennedy took it over in 1952. It is still  in good condition, however, many of the interior furnishings have been removed. In more recent years the trading post included a laundromat, which the current owner hopes to reopen along with the store.

History: The post was started by George Sampson in 1890 and sold to Percy Craig in 1892, followed by Lorenzo Haskell from 1898 to 1908. The next owner of record was Albert Arnold who acquired it around 1913. Following Arnolds' death the ownership was transferred to his son Albert Arnold, Jr., along with his daughter and her husband, Glen Williams, and another daughter. In 1946, Albert Arnold, Jr. and Al Tietjen became the owners with Tietjen assuming ownership in 1949. He was followed by Walter and Troy Kennedy (1952), Charlie Lee (1957), Raymond Carson (1959), and Samuel Christensen (1971). Christensen closed the store in 1985 and turned the business and lease over to James Nakai, who still has plans to reopen.

Mexican Springs Trading Post*

Located about 5 miles south of Tohatchi and 3.5 miles west of US 491 on NR 30 (last .6 mile is gravel).

Description: *Abandoned.* A fire in July 2004 ended the existence of a very authentic, old trading post. The remains of the main building along with adjacent wooden structures, have been cleaned up, and all  that survives is a small pile of stones, barely enough to indicate where the post once stood. The main building that housed the store had the external appearance of an old-time trading post. It was made out of cut stone and had frame additions on each end that were used as residences. After the most recent owner took over, the store's interior was rearranged and no longer had the old trading post atmosphere or appearance. The shelves lining the walls and the wood counters forming the bullpen were removed, as was the old pot-bellied stove that occupied the center of the room. Outside there was a low storage building reported to have been built using wood from old army ammunition boxes. The calvary from Fort Robinson used the site as a stopping area during the Beautiful Mountain Uprising.

History: The original post was started by Edward Vanderwagen in 1916, however, it is believed that the last building, which was made of stone, had its origin around 1939. Information on subsequent owners is unavailable until John Soper in the late 1940s, followed by his manager Ernie Garcia. Others included Eddie Yonkers in 1950, Clifford Miller in 1963, and Leslie Phillips, Jr. in 1983. The last owner, Cora Johnson, took it over in 1995.

Coyote Canyon Trading Post*

Located on NR 9, 9.4 miles west of US 491 and .1 mile south of the highway.

Description: *Closed.* This authentic trading post was closed in November, 2001 with the hopes of reopenng, but it is very doubtful that will ever happen. The building in which the store was housed is made of cut red sandstone and is in fairly good condition. The store  interior had an old-time, rustic appearance, but it actually functioned as a small self-service grocery store and did not carry any arts and crafts. It has an attractive location just off NR 9, which is one of the more scenic drives on the reservation.

History: George Sampson started the post in 1896 and sold it to Dan DuBois in 1902. Claude Powell became the owner in 1937. John Kirk owned it from 1945 until around 1948 when Harold and Meleta Brimhall took it over and subsequently formed a partnership with Willard and Wilda Brimhall in 1950. Following Willard Brimhall's death in 1961,

Wilda Brimhall and Bruce McLaws, Wilda's son-in-law, became the sole owners. They sold it to Thriftway Corp. in 1980, at which time it quit functioning as a trading post. A female clerk was murdered in the store in January, 1998, which resulted in a drop in business among the local Navajo population. The more traditional Navajos believe a building in which a person has died could have a chindi (death spirit) and will not enter it. Since its closing the building has been vacant and is gradually deteriorating.

OTHER ABANDONED TRADING POSTS

■ **Elmer Foutz Store:** It is located across the road from the old Fruitland post office. It was started by Elmer Foutz around 1944 and closed by him in the late 1950s. The building is still present and in fair condition.

■ **Southside:** It is located .7 mile west of the old Fruitland post office. It was started by Bob Martin around 1932, followed by Ira Hatch and Charlie Ashcroft in 1934 and Jack Cline, 1939 to 1948. An old building in poor condition remains.

■ **Westwater:** It was located north and east of the Hogback ridge. The post was established in 1897 or '98 by Joseph Hatch and Edgar Thurland. It was closed by them around 1902 and was subsequently demolished for building materials. Only the outline of the foundation remains.

■ **Cove:** To reach Cove, turn onto NR 63 one-half mile before Red Rock Trading Post. Go .3 mile and turn left onto NR 33 for 12.3 miles to the site. The post was established by Wendell Reid, a Navajo and followed by Nelson Jack and Willard Leighton (1955), Jewel McGee and Troy Kennedy (1958), and Troy Kennedy (1966). He closed it in 1989 and

the lease reverted to the Navajo tribe. Calvin Adair, who worked for Kennedy, attempted to run it for a couple years, but closed it for good in 1991. It has been torn down, the site cleaned up, and no trace of the store remains. Cove Mesa Arch, a large, attractive stone arch, is located just northwest of Cove. To drive to it, obtain directions locally.

■ **Sehili:** Its site was not located, but the approximate location was twenty-five miles southeast of Round Rock Trading Post. It was established by Stephen Aldrich & Elias Clark in 1884, with Charles Hubbell, Lorenzo's younger brother, as their clerk. It then sold to Archibald Sweetland in 1889 and was closed by him in 1892.

■ **Sulphur Springs:** The site was not located, but was approximately thirty-one miles south of Shiprock and 1/4 mile east of US 491. It was established by Alison Miller in 1888. Stephen Booten took it over in 1889 and abandoned it in 1891.

■ **Tocito:** It was located on NR 56, a graded dirt road, 3.3 miles west of US 491. This junction is 24.3 miles south of Shiprock. It was destroyed shortly after it closed and only portions of two walls remain. The post was established by Jess Foutz and Sante Bowen in 1913. Other owners included Melvin McGee, Joe Tanner, Russell Foutz, Pete Corey, and Phil Foutz. R. B. Foutz, Jr., took it over around 1983 and closed it in 1985. The original license for Tocito, which means "warm water" in Navajo, was issued by Shiprock Agency Superintendent William Shelton in

Melvin and Bessie McGee behind counter at Tocito Trading post, 1955. (Photo courtesy of Grace Herring)

order to cut into the trading business of Frank Noel's Sanostee store located only seven miles away. Shelton was angry with Noel because of a disagreement between them involving the Beautiful Mountain Uprising. Noel, who had been dealing with the Navajos, refused to tell Shelton the location of Bizhoshi and about a dozen other Navajos who were hiding on Beautiful Mountain. (See Sanostee Trading Post)

■ **Burnham:** It was located on NR 5 about 12.3 miles east of its junction with US 491. It was started by Roy Burnham in 1927, followed by Roy's son Bob Burnham and Roy Foutz (1939), Melvin McGee (1944), Wayne Brimhall (1955), and Roscoe and Kelly McGee in 1958. They closed it around 1962. The original building was a relatively small, wooden structure. In 1972, the building was demolished and hauled away by locals for building materials and firewood. Part of it was used for warming fires during one of the AIM (American Indian Movement) demonstrations in the area.

Roy Burnham packing wool into a sack at Burham Trading Post, about 1918. (Photo courtesy of Fern Duckworth)

■ **Newcomb: (Also known as Nava)** It was located on US 491, 35.5 miles south of Shiprock. It was established by John L. Oliver around 1904. Subsequent owners were Charles Nelson (1911), Arthur Newcomb (1913), Marshall Drolet and Paul Brink (1951), Paul Brink (1962), and R. B. Foutz, Jr. (1980-2003). The post was originally located in a small log cabin, which was moved in the early 1900s, and subsequently replaced with a cinder-block building by the last owner. It was destroyed by fire in April, 2003 and nothing remains. The store developed into a very successful trading business under Newcomb's ownership and high quality blankets and rugs were produced from the area. It was a very popular place in its early days and was visited by various dignitaries including the Crown Prince of Sweden.

■ **Black Salt:** The site was not located, but was approximately five miles west of Crystal Trading Post. It was established by Stephen Aldrich & Elias Clark in 1882 and closed in 1883.

■ **Buffalo Springs:** It was located on the west side of US 491, 9.2 miles north of Tohatchi. It was started by a Navajo in 1946 and sold to Eddy Yonkers in the early 1950s, followed by Willard Leighton and Nelson Jack (1957), Nelson Jack (1958), and Jack Davin (1959). The Navajo tribe took it over in the late '60s and closed it. Nothing remains.

■ **Tuye Springs (Chaco Trading Co.):** It was located on US 491, 2.3 miles north of the its junction with NM 264. It was established by James Bennett & Volney Edie in 1889 and closed in 1892. A later post at the same site **(called Tohlakai)** was built by Howard Wilson around 1938 and sold to Claude Powell in 1946, followed by Phil Foutz in 1959. A Thriftway store has occupied the site since the early 1980s.

■ **China Springs:** It was located three miles south of the US 491 and NM 264 junction. It was established in 1906 by a party unknown. Other owners included Frank Maple (1910), J. J. Phillips (1911), and Frank "Sloppy Jack" Lewis (1915). Lewis was murdered at the post in 1921. He was followed by Shanty Meyers (early '30s), Jack Powell (1954), and Charlie Ashcroft (1955). The post was closed about a year later. An old building is still present. China Springs was the scene of a U.S. cavalry ambush by the Navajos in 1863.

Chapter 5

Chinle

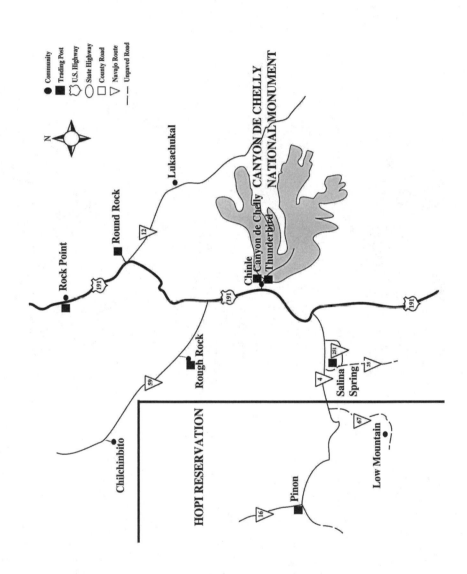

Rock Point Trading Post★★
P. O. Box 157, Rock Point, AZ 86545, (928) 659-4329

Located on US 191, 15.4 miles south of the US 191/US 160 junction.

Description: *Converted.* The trading post has been in continuous operation since it started. It still does occasional trading, but is mainly operated as a gas and grocery convenience store and retains little of the functions of the old-time trading post that it once was. The old, red sandstone building that housed the original trading post is still located next to the current store. It is in fairly good condition and is preserved as a historical site. On the other side of the store are a post office and laundromat. The building the current store is housed in was built in 1978 and renovated in 1987. It has brown metal siding with a stone veneer across the front and a nearly flat metal roof. The store appears to be quite busy, and there is much activity around it, partly due to the presence of the post office and laundromat.

History: The origin of this post is uncertain, but it is believed that a party by the name of Zinn may have started it around 1910. Ray Dunn acquired it in 1925 and was followed by George and Dan Christensen (1927), Karl Ashcroft and Sylvan "Curly" Jack (1937), Vernon Bloomfield and Sylvan Jack (1946), Raymond Blair (1948) with Arville Witt as a partner (1949), and Bob Cook (1976). The current owner is Giant Industries which took it over in 1991.

Round Rock Trading Post★★★★
P. O. Box DD, Round Rock, AZ 86547, (928) 787-2489

Located on a gravel road .2 mile east of US 191; turnoff is just north of the US 191 and NR 12 junction.

Description: *Original.* Although the trading post is basically operated as a small self-service grocery store, it is still located in the original building, has not been significantly renovated or modernized either inside or out, and is quite quaint and authentic in appearance. In addition to gas and groceries, it carries general merchandise, buys and sells a limited amount of Indian arts and crafts, and does occasional trading. The original building was made of thick stone walls with vegas supporting a flat roof. It has a cinder block addition on the front, which is painted white. The floor of the original bullpen was covered with boards from Arbuckles coffee crates.

History: Round Rock is the oldest licensed trading post still in operation on the reservation. It was started in 1887 by Stephen Aldrich, a former cavalryman and veteran of the Apache campaigns, and Chee Dodge. Chee Dodge, the first Navajo Tribal Chairman when the Tribal Council formed in 1923, was the son of a Mexican man and a Navajo woman. He was named after Col. Henry Dodge. Chee, which means red, was a nickname given him by soldiers and Indians around Fort Defiance where he grew up. He died in 1946 at the age of 86.

Aldrich and Dodge were followed by C. N. Cotton in 1911. Owners following Cotton were short-term and unsuccessful. Ownership reverted back to Cotton, who closed the post for several years until Vernon Jack and Karl Ashcroft took it over in 1933. Ashcroft assumed full ownership in 1940 and sold it to Vernon Bloomfield and Bud Foutz in 1945. They were followed by Vernon and Sylvan Jack (1946), Henry Reynolds (1948), Raymond Blair (1949), C. E. Wheeler (1976), Thriftway Corp. (1988), Giant Industries (2000), and the current owner Richard Yazzie, who acquired it in August, 2001.

The post was the site of the famous Black Horse Rebellion of 1892, which occurred when Indian agent David Shipley was taken hostage by Black Horse and a number of well-armed followers. They were upset because of Shipley's cruel and deceitful methods of luring Indian children to the Fort Defiance boarding school, a place notorious for mistreatment and unhealthy conditions. Chee Dodge and trader Charles Hubbard rescued Shipley from being beaten to death, and they all took refuge in the store. The siege lasted for two days and ended with the arrival of a dozen soldiers summoned from Sehili. A Navajo policeman had slipped away from the confrontation, and found the soldiers twenty-three miles away.

Rough Rock Trading Post★★★★
HC 61, Box 5000, Chinle, AZ 86503, (928) 728-3252

> *Go west on NR 59 13.3 miles from its junction with US 191; turn left onto NR 8066 and go 2.4 miles to NR 59G; turn left for .2 mile to end of pavement.*

Description: *Original.* The present trading post was built in the 1930s. It is constructed of native cut stone and has an attached residence. It was remodeled in the 1950s, at which time the residence was enlarged and improved. A fire occured at some later date after which a new metal roof was installed over the entire building. The building appears to be in good condition, and has a very authentic appearance. The interior still has some of the old furnishings and has the atmosphere of an old-time store. In addition to groceries, it sells hardware, ranch supplies, and other general merchandise, and maintains the local post office. It still

Current Rough Rock Trading Post, 2003

carries on limited trading, primarily for local Navajo rugs and jewelry. The post is located at the end of a dirt road in a box canyon surrounded by low rocky bluffs. It presents a very rustic setting.

History: The original trading post was established by Clitso Dedman around 1897 and was probably started in a tent and later moved into the small rectangular stone structure located about twenty yards west of the current store. Andrea Ashcroft, a recent owner, did some research on the original post and started its restoration. She stated that an elderly resident of the area told her the original trading post did not have a bullpen (where trading is normally carried on), and that it was more of a wareroom or warehouse with trade carried on thru a window

Original Rough Rock Trading Post as it appeared in 2003.

Rough Rock Trading Post in 1939, shortly after it was built to replace the original. (Photo courtesy of Don Shillingburg)

located in the front of the building. A bullpen may have been added later on, and it was definately included when the current store was built.

Joe Gallena acquired the post around 1916 and sold it to Con Shillingburg in 1919. He was followed by Lon and Clarence Wheeler with Troy Washburn as a partner (1946), Gus Farr (1973), Raymond Carson (1984), Al Grieve (1986), Phil Foutz (1989), and Preston Thayne (1990). It was closed from 1993 until 1996 when Andrea Ashcroft reopened it. She subsequently sold it to the current owner, Bonnie Jackson, in 2003.

Canyon de Chelly Trading Post★★
P. O. Box 1889, Chinle, AZ 86503, (928) 674-5000

Located on NR 7, one-half mile west of Canyon de Chelly National Monument Visitor Center in Chinle, AZ.

Description: *Converted.* This post was also known as **Garcia Trading Post**. The site where it was located is currently occupied by the Holiday Inn Motel. The old trading post building itself has been remodeled and houses a gift shop and restaurant that are part of the motel.

History: The first trading operations in the Chinle area were improvised affairs run out of tents. Little Mexican, or "Nakai Yazzie" as the Navajos called him, started a store in 1882 at the mouth of Canyon de

Chelly, which lasted about a year. The first permanent trading post in the Chinle area was established at the site where the Canyon de Chelly Trading Post would eventually be located. It was started in 1885 by J. Lorenzo Hubbell and C. N. Cotton. They took over an abandoned stone hogan, added three rooms of hand-hewn rock, and a floor made from Arbuckles coffee crates. Apparently business was not too good as Hubbell and Cotton failed to renew their license after their first year. In 1914, Hubbell built a second post a few miles west of the original site. It was a large two-story stone building. In addition to a trading post, he intended to use the second floor to house guests touring the area. He was a little premature with this idea and, in 1917, sold out to his partner C. N. Cotton. This store was bought out around 1923 by the partnership of Camille Garcia, Leon "Cozy" McSparron, and Hartley Seymour.

A series of traders followed Hubbell and Cotton at the site of their original post and, sometime during this period of ownership, the old hogan post was replaced by a red corrugated metal building. In 1912, John Kirk took over the post, and a new, larger stone trading post and trader's residence were built. The partnership of Garcia, McSparron, and Seymour bought the store in 1920, and Garcia subsequently bought out the other two partners. He then enlarged the trading post and added additional buildings, plus a gas pump and a rock hut for Navajo visitors. After World War II, the post developed into more of a self-service store and gas station and was the first of its kind in the Chinle area. The trading post, which was named Canyon de Chelly Trading Post by Garcia, served as a post office, bank, and general center for the Chinle community.

In 1962, Camille Garcia and his son Abel were killed in a plane crash at the Chinle airstrip. The Garcia family continued to operate the post until 1985, when it was closed it. An employee continued to occupy the site until 1988. Shortly after that, the buildings began to be badly vandalized. The site was subsequently cleared (except for the actual trading post building and old residence currently occupied by the motel manager), and the 100-room Holiday Inn motel was built in 1992.

Thunderbird Lodge★★★
P. O. Box 548, Chinle, AZ 86503, (928) 674-5841

Located inside Canyon de Chelly National Monument, .6 mile past the Visitors Center.

Description: *Converted.* Thunderbird Lodge, the successor to the original trading post that occupied the site, consists of a very attractive modern motel, a cafeteria with an excellent display of Navajo rugs on the walls and an adjoining artifacts room, and an Indian arts and crafts store. The cafeteria is located in the original 1902 trading post building.

History: The original trading post, located a short distance from the mouth of Canyon de Chelly, was a sturdy log structure built by Samuel E. Day in 1902. Day sold out to Charles F. Weidemeyer in 1905, who sold it to John Kirk in 1909, followed by George Kennedy in 1916. In 1919, Cozy McSparron, with Camille Garcia and Hartley Seymour as partners, bought the post from Kennedy. Cozy then bought out the other two partners in 1925 and began running it as a combination trading post and dude ranch, renaming it Thunderbird Lodge. Cozy continued to run it until 1954, when he sold out to John Nelson. Nelson died five years later, and his widow managed it until 1964 when Gerald LaFont purchased it. At this point it ceased functioning as a trading post, with

Historic Thunderbird Lodge in 1902, back when it operated as a trading post. (Museum of New Mexico, #15988)

LaFont building the first motel units and concentrating on the tourist business. In 1984, he sold it to Mary Jones, the current owner, who has continued to develop the lodge and has added additional motel units.

A good general rug is produced in the Chinle area. It is distinctive and well woven, but does not have as fine a weave as the Wide Ruins area rugs. Vegetal dye Yei rugs are also made in the Chinle area.

Salina Springs Trading Post★★

Take US 191 south from Chinle for 3.3 miles; turn right onto NR 4 for 14.4 miles, then left onto NR 251 for 3.3 miles.

Description: *Abandoned.* In 2002, the Navajo Tribe tore down all the buildings and cleared the area. A large metal building, used as a nursery or day school, currently occupies the site. Until it was torn down, the trading post, barn, and corrals were in relatively good condition. However, it is doubtful that this interesting old post would ever have reopened. Nonetheless, it is unfortunate that this post closed. Not too many years ago, it was one of the most quaint, authentic, and colorful posts on the reservation, with a location to match. The exterior of the store had not changed much, but many of the interior furnishings had

Old Salina Springs Trading post in 1998, prior to its removal.

been removed or damaged. Even with it closed, a visit to this old post is worthwhile just to see the old buildings and the scenic area in which it was located.

History: The post was established in 1913 by George Kennedy. Horace and Harry Boardman bought it in 1915 and sold it about two years later to William Bickel and Lewis Sabin. Lester Lee acquired a half interest in 1924 and later bought out Bickel and Sabin. Albert Lee, Lester's brother, subsequently assumed ownership and then, in 1949, turned it over to his son Arthur, who ran it until he sold it to Dave Murray in 1962. Murray's son was shot and killed at the post in 1987, as was the next owner, Alex Todd, who took it over from Murray in 1990 and ran it until his death in 1992. Joe Cline acquired it that same year. Cline's daughter and husband, Janni and Wilbert Yazzie, tried running it for a year, but business had fallen off sharply after the unfortunate incidents. They turned it back to Joe Cline in 1994. He closed it about a year later, and it reverted to the Navajo tribe.

Pinon Trading Post★★
P. O. Box 437, Pinon, AZ 86510, (928) 725-3335

Located just south of NR 4, about 35 miles west of its junction with US 191.

Description: *Closed.* Unfortunately, this historic old post was closed in January, 2003. Competition from a large, modern grocery store had forced changes in the operation, and it no longer functioned quite like the old trading post it once was. There was a time during the 1960s when Pinon was the largest volume store on the Navajo Reservation. It was still located in the original building, a large rock structure with a full basement that, in the early days, held wagon loads of store supplies. Back then, the roads were impassable most of the winter and all freight was brought in by wagon during the summer months. The original building has been greatly enlarged, remodeled, and modernized. In addition to groceries, the post sold hardware, auto supplies, and other general merchandise. It also had a cafe, laundromat, and car wash. It also sold excellent Indian arts and crafts, including rugs from the Ganado, Klagetoh, Burnwater, Dinnebito, and Chinle areas.

History: Established by Lorenzo Hubbell in 1916. Lorenzo Hubbell, Jr., operated the store for his father, as did his cousin George Hubbell. Ed Thatcher was also involved and may have had a part interest in it, since the store was called **Thatcher's Trading Post** during the period around 1928. The Navajo tribe took over the post in 1951 and operated

Pinon Trading Post shortly before closing in 2003.

it under a series of managers until 1954, when C. E. Wheeler and Bill McGee became the owners. The next year Cliff McGee, Bill's brother, joined the partnership. In 1961 Wheeler sold out, leaving Bill and Cliff McGee as the owners. Cliff and his sons took over ownership in 1972, and Cliff's son Ferron ran it until its recent closing.

OTHER ABANDONED TRADING POSTS

■ **Lukachukai:** It was located about 100 yards north of NR 13, one mile from its junction with NR 12. It was established by George Barker in 1892, followed by George Sampson (about 1900), W. R. Cassidy (1916), Earl Kennedy (1928), and Earl's son Kenneth Kennedy from 1971 until it closed in 1979. The place was demolished after it closed because of a rumor that there was cash hidden at various places in the building. It was later torn down and only rubble from the foundation remains. A newer store, **Totsoh Trading Post** operated by Hank and Victoria Blair, is located about a mile farther down the road.

■ **Upper Greasewood:** It was located on an unmarked dirt road .2 mile east of NR 12; the turnoff is three miles south of the Lukachukai Road. Oscar Marty established the post in 1911, followed by J. H. McAdams. Burt Dustin owned it in 1924 with John Wade having a part interest. They were followed by Karl Ashcroft (1932), Clinton and Merrill Taylor (1933), Don Shillingburg (1942), and Prat Nelson (1953). The last owner, C. E. Wheeler, acquired it in 1961 and closed it in 1982. It burned down shortly afterward and only a cement slab remains. A near tragic event occurred when Oscar Marty owned the post. He got into a dispute with a Navajo concerning ten cents the Navajo claimed was owed him. Marty stubbornly refused to pay. The Navajo returned later that night and fired a .30-.30 rifle through the window, hitting Marty's clerk in the shoulder and grazing his son's head. A second shot missed completely. Marty promptly sold the post and left the country.

■ **Many Farms Store:** It was located at the junction of US 191 and NR 59. It was originally called **Red Ridge** when it was established as a co-op by Navajos in 1945. It was sold to Wallace Anderson in 1948, followed by Glen Osterfeld and Keith Redd, who sold it in the early '80s. Fina built a replacement store in 1991 and sold it to Giant in 1993. Only a cement slab remains of the original store.

■ **Chilchinbeto:** It was located thirteen miles south of US 160 on NR 59 and two miles in from the highway. Started by Lee Bradley in 1906, other owners included George Sampson (1910), Ray Dunn, Howard Wilson, and Camillo Garcia (1930), Melvin McGee (1938), Ray Hunt (1944), Glen Heflin (1956), Ray Hunt again in 1963, Sam Christensen (1964), Robert Walker (1983), and Phil & Brian Foutz who closed it in 1990. It burned down in 1992 and only the ruins of the foundation are left.

Chilchinbeto Trading Post, 1949. (Photo courtesy of Stewart Hatch)

■ **Valley Store:** It was located on US 191, ten miles north of Chinle. It was started by Tom Frazier in the early 1900s, sold to Carmillo Garcia in 1934, and closed around 1978. Nothing remains.

■ **Black Mountain:** It was located 4.6 miles up NR 25A from its junction with NR 4 and .5 mile west of the road. The original post was started in 1914 by Lorenzo Hubbell. Win Wetherill operated it in 1916; other operators included Joe Lee and Miles Hedrick. Albert Lee bought the post in 1937. Albert's son, Arthur Lee, took it over in the late 1940s, closed it in 1963, and it burned down in 1975. Only a cement slab and rubble from the foundation remains.

■ **Low Mountain:** It was located on NR 67, 13.2 miles in from NR 4. It was started by Joseph Schmedding around 1920. E. P. Halderman was the next owner in 1924. Albert Lee owned it in the late '40s, Joe Danoff in 1959, and it closed in 1985. The original building was made of stone with a corrugated metal roof. Some stone rubble remains.

■ **Round Valley:** It is located about 1/4 mile east of Pinon Trading Post. It was started by Clifford Beck in 1935. Subsequent owners included Phil, Keith & Cal Foutz, Golden Gallager and J. B. Collyer (referred to as the Foutz Trading Co.) in 1954, followed by Sylvan Jack and Wilford Guillory in 1962. It went back to Beck in 1970 and remained closed until 1987. It reopened for a short time and then closed for good in 1992. The building is still standing and in fair condition.

■ **Big Mountain:** It was located in a remote section of the Hopi reservation about twenty miles northwest of Pinon. The original post was started by Lorenzo Hubbell, Jr. in 1935, who was replaced by Golden Nelson around 1946 for Albert Lee. Lee was unable to obtain a lease from the tribe, and the store was closed about two or three years later. It was of log construction, and nothing remains at the site.

Chapter 6

Window Rock

FT. DEFIANCE TRDG CO '76

Abraham J. Tucker

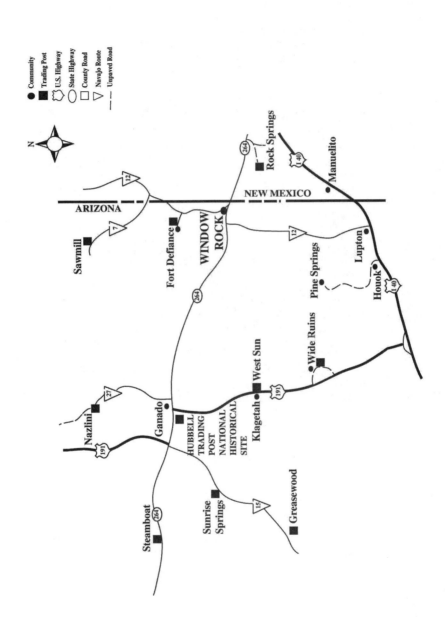

Rock Springs Trading Post★★

708 East Aztec, Gallup, NM 87301, (505) 371-5744

Go 2.7 miles west on NM 264 from its junction with US 491; turn south on Rock Spring Rd. for .7 mile to turnoff at Wilson Ranch sign, then 2.6 miles on gravel and dirt road to the site.

Description: *Abandoned:* The old trading post was originally in a separate stone building. Later on, a residence was constructed adjacent to it. The two buildings were subsequently joined together by Larry Wilson in 1972 when he enclosed the space between them to form one large structure. The old trading post portion is used to house a private museum containing an interesting collection of early western artifacts and memorabilia. The remainder forms a large residence. The museum has been visited by people from all over the United States and several countries. The owner asks anyone wishing to visit the museum to please call first.

History: Dan Dubois started trading in this area, which is off the reservation, out of a crude tent-store in the early 1860s. It was probably the first and only trading operation in the region at the time. The Navajos were moved to Bosque Redondo in 1864. It was four years before they returned, so business may have been slow for awhile. The old wagon road between Fort Wingate and Fort Defiance passed near the post, no doubt providing some occasional business and company. The post was sold in 1887 to George Sampson who constructed the stone structure that is still in existence. George Kennedy acquired it in 1921 and operated it until 1935 when Gallup Mercantile took it over and subsequently closed the old post.

Fort Defiance Trading Post**

From Window Rock, AZ go 4.4 miles north on NR 12 to stop light; do not turn on NR 12, but go straight ahead toward Fort Defiance for 1.5 miles to the site, which is on the left side of the road.

Description: *Abandoned.* The trading post was housed in a large rectangular stone building over 100 feet long and 50 feet wide, similiar to the old Hubbell Trading Post building. Unfortunately, it was torn down around 1995. The site was subsequently cleaned up and nothing remains — the site is now an empty lot. There is nothing left of either the old fort or the trading post, but there are many historic old buildings in Fort Defiance, and it is an interesting area to visit.

History: The year and name of the party who started the post is uncertain. Some of the early licensed traders at Fort Defiance were Perry Williams in 1877, William Leonard in 1880, and Billy Weidemeyer in 1891. Subsequent owners were Charles Manning (1896), Ilfeld Trading Co. (1906), William Bickel (1908), Hans Neumann (1912), Lew Sabin (1915), W. M. Staggs (1933), Vic Walker (1955), and R. B. Foutz, Jr. (1978). The post closed around 1983. The first post office in the Territory of Arizona was located in the trading post.

Overlooking Fort Defiance Trading Post, 1963. Roof of Dunn Mercantile in foreground. (Photo courtesy of Earl Ashcroft)

Navajos gather for Fort Defiance's annual Christmas party. When the
crowd got too large inside store, candy was tossed from the roof, 1963.
(Photo courtesy of Earl Ashcroft)

Fort Defiance, the first U. S. Army post in Arizona, was established
in 1851 by Colonel Edwin Sumner. For defensive purposes it was located
at the end of a box canyon known as Bonito Canyon. The fort was
abandoned at the start of the Civil War and deteriorated badly. Because
of increased Navajo raiding on settlers, the fort was reopened in 1863 and
renamed Fort Canby, after the commander of the New Mexico militia.
The first licensed trading post on the reservation was at Fort Defiance in
1868, after the Navajos returned from Bosque Redondo. It was started in
the abandoned adobe and log buildings of the old fort when the military
garrison pulled out. One of the first traders was a German immigrant
named Lehman Spiegelberg who was there in 1868 when the Navajos
returned. Ansom Damon started a post around 1869, named **Black Rock**,
located just south of Fort Defiance. Lorenzo Hubbell, in partnership with
Henry Reed, established a post there in 1873. Also in 1873, Thomas
Keam started his Fairview post located a few miles south of Fort
Defiance. Others who operated posts in the Fort Defiance area included
Romulo Martinez in 1873; Ben Hyatt in 1881; Hyatt's clerk, Sam Reeder,
who took over Hyatt's store in 1885; Walter Fales, Keam's manager,
in 1884; Michael Donavan in 1885; and John Weidemeyer in 1886.

Sawmill Trading Post
P. O. Box 8, Sawmill, AZ 86549

Take NR 12 north out of Window Rock for 6.7 miles to second stop light; turn left and follow NR 7 for 13.8 miles to Tsosie Dr. in center of community of Sawmill; turn right for 1/8 mile to trading post.

Description: *Closed.* The post was remodeled before it closed, but no longer functioned as a trading post. It has a reddish-tan colored stucco exterior with vegas extending out the front near the roofline. The front of the building is very plain without any name or sign on it and no windows or openings other than the door. The store served the local Navajo population, selling gas, groceries, and general merchandise, and operating a small post office.

History: The post is believed to have been started by John Taylor around 1910, followed by John Staggs and his step-son, Gene Baird in the late 1930's; Bill Palmer and Troy Washburn; the Navajo Tribe; and Foutz Trading Co. in 1957. The next owner, Evan Lewis, took it over in 1971 and turned it over to his son who closed it in 2002. Business greatly dropped off when the sawmill closed and moved to Navajo, NM in 1963. It is doubtful the store will ever reopen.

Nazlini Trading Post★

P. O. Box 7391, Nazlini, AZ 86540, (928) 755-3044

Located on NR 27 about 17 miles north of AZ 264; go left just before Chapter House onto the old gravel road for .4 mile.

Description: *Closed.* The old post went through a lot of changes after it was first established. When it no longer functioned as a trading post, it operated as a typical gas and grocery convenience store. It was located in an attractive part of the reservation. The gravel and dirt road beyond the post leads to Canyon de Chelly National Monument.

History: The post was established by Lorenzo Hubbell in 1911 and operated by his son Lorenzo Hubbell, Jr.. Subsequent owners were Tom Shillingburg (1923), Fred Carson (1937), Prat Nelson (1945), Hugh Lee (1953), J. B. Tanner (1954), Art Lee (1955), Troy Washburn (1956), David Goff (1957), Francis Griswold (1958), Fred (Allen) Carson (1972), Lon Farmer (1981), Magar Singh (1983), Thriftway Corp. (1989), Giant Industries (2000), and the current owner, Shirley Bydonnie, in August, 2001.

Hubbell Trading Post★★★★

P. O. Box 388, Ganado, AZ 86505, (928) 755-3254

Located just south of AZ 264, about 1/2 mile west of Ganado, AZ.

Description: *Original.* The trading post is still housed in the original building, which is a large, rectangular structure constructed of reddish

Hubbell Trading Post, 1999

Hubbell Trading Post interior, 1999

sandstone rocks gathered from the surrounding hills. The building is thick-walled with iron-barred windows and high, beamed ceilings. In addition to the store, there is an adjoining wareroom where merchandise and trade goods were stored. Next to the store are a large stone barn and corrals. Immediately behind the trading post is Hubbell's old adobe house, built in 1902, where tours are currently conducted. Also out back are a guest hogan, bread oven, chicken coop, and stone bunkhouse.

The interior of the trading post has not changed much since the 1940s. It consists of the bullpen, jewelry room, and rug room. The bullpen is the main room where groceries, fabric, tack, and other merchandise can be purchased. It contains the original wooden floors, shelves, counters, and display cases used in the early trading days. General merchandise can be seen packed on shelves and hanging from ceiling beams, which has been the custom for years. Visitors can see a truly authentic old-time trading post where trade with the Navajos is carried on now as it was over a half century ago.

History: The original post in the area was started by Charles Crary in 1871. He sold out to William "Old Man" Leonard in 1875. Lorenzo Hubbell purchased Leonard's post in 1878, immediately built a larger building next to it, and, in 1883, began building the current trading post which was completed in 1889. In 1882, Hubbell was elected sheriff of Apache County and resided at St Johns, AZ. He needed someone to look after his affairs at Ganado, so in 1884 he took on C. N. Cotton as a one-half partner. A year later he turned the post over to Cotton while he completed two terms as sheriff, followed by participation in the Territorial Legislature. Their partnership lasted until 1894, after which they remained good friends.

Following Hubbell's death in 1930 at the age of seventy-six, the trading post was passed on to his sons Lorenzo, Jr. and Roman. Both sons continued the trading business — Lorenzo, Jr. until his death in 1943 and Roman until his death in 1957. Roman and his wife Dorothy continued to run the trading post as absentee owners and later lived at the post. After Roman passed away, operating the post became too much for Dorothy. She eventually sold the post and the extensive collection of artifacts to the U. S. Government in 1967 for $300,000 with a stipulation that the post remain an active trading post. It has been designated a

A view of the inside of the warehouse where furs, supplies, and general merchandise were stored, about 1890. (Courtesy of NPS Museum, Hubbell Trading Post National Historic Site, #HUTR-2178)

Lorenzo Hubbell, seated, examining a rug with Navajo woman in foreground and trading post in background, 1890. (Museum of New Mexico, #16480)

Hubbell Trading Post, 1890, showing the main entrance to the store. (Museum of New Mexico, #47913)

Juan Lorenzo Hubbell, 1910. (Courtesy of NPS Museum, Hubbell Trading Post National Historic Site, #HUTR 4709)

Hubbell Trading Post warehouse and barn, 1999.

National Historical Site and is administered by the National Park Service. Since its sale, the post was under the management of Billy Young until 1979, followed by Al Grieve from 1979 to 1982, and Bill Malone from 1982 to 2005. Steven Pickle has managed the post since 2005.

Hubbell Trading Post is the oldest continuously operated trading post within the Navajo reservation, and one of the first to be established outside the Fort Defiance area. The land on which it is located was claimed by Hubbell under the 1862 Homestead Act and comprised 160 acres. When the Navajo reservation was expanded in 1880, his trading post was included and was to become part of the reservation. Hubbell was determined not to have that happen. After several hearings requiring trips to Washington and Phoenix, and through assistance from influential men such as Arizona's governor, he was able to eventually get Congress to pass a bill allowing his claim based on "prior rights." His homestead patent was finally issued in 1917. The area around the trading post was formally known as Pueblo Colorado. Because of confusion with the town of Pueblo, Colorado, Hubbell had the name changed to Ganado in honor of his friend Ganado Mucho ("Many Herds").

Juan Lorenzo Hubbell was born in Pajarito, New Mexico in 1853, son of a Connecticut Yankee and a Spanish mother. He was often addressed as Don Lorenzo, a Spanish title of respect, and was called Nakai Sani ("old Mexican") or Nak'ee sinili ("double glasses") by the Navajos. He was well liked by the Indians, treated them fairly, and encouraged the development of their arts and crafts. He expanded his Indian trading business to include more than twenty-four other trading posts on or around the reservation and two wholesale stores. He also ran a freighting business and issued mail-order catalogs. His interest went far beyond the reservation. He was sheriff of Apache County for four years, a territorial representative, one of Arizona's first elected state senators, and ran unsuccessfully for the U. S. Senate. His hacienda was host to many artists, writers, and politicians of the time, including President Theodore Roosevelt. Hubbell died on November 12, 1930, and was buried on Hubbell Hill overlooking the trading post. With him are buried his wife Lina Rubi, his two sons, a daughter Adele, and his Navajo friend "Many Horses," Granado Mucho's son.

Steamboat Trading Post

HCR 58, Box 40, Ganado, AZ 86505, (928) 736-2586

Located on AZ 264, 20.3 miles west of Ganado.

Description: *Converted.* The post has been converted into a modern gas and grocery convenience store and no longer functions as a trading post. The previous location of the post was about 100 feet to the east in a large metal quonset hut with a cinder block addition. It is still standing. The original post was located behind the current store. Only stone rubble remains.

History: The post's origin is uncertain. It is likely Lorenzo Hubbell started it since he is known to have owned it from 1912 to around 1917. Subsequent owners included Albert Lee in 1935 and Lester Lee in 1940. The store burned in 1952. It was rebuilt and operated by Jerold Foutz in 1955 and the Navajo tribe in 1984. Thriftway took it over in 1987, followed by current owner Red Mesa Express in 1989.

Sunrise Springs Trading Post★

Located just off NR 15, 12.5 miles south of AZ 264. The NR 15/AZ 264 junction is 6 miles west of Ganado.

Description: *Abandoned.* This post was originally housed in a large, attractive building with a white painted stucco exterior. The walls are still standing, but most of the roof is missing and the interior has been destroyed.

Remains of Sunrise Springs Trading Post, 1999.

History: The post was established by J. H. McAdams and E. J. Marty in 1907. Shortly after, Lorenzo Hubbell informed them that they were operating in his trading territory and ordered them to leave. Marty moved to Gallup, but McAdams defiantly stayed on and bought Marty out. In 1909, he sold out to his nephew, Hubert Richardson. William Bickel Co. bought the post around 1920. Albert Lee acquired a half interest in 1924 and then, along with partner Clarence Wheeler, bought out Bickel in 1929. Subsequent owners were Clarence Wheeler and Harold Springer in the early 1940s, and Jay Springer and Gene Wheeler in early 1970s. It closed in 1987.

Greasewood Trading Post
1 Hickman Blvd., Indian Wells, AZ 86031, (928) 654-3302

> *Located about .2 mile west of NR 15 and 20.7 miles south of the NR 15/AZ 264 junction, which is 6 mile west of Ganado.*

Description: *Converted.* The store, which no longer functions as a trading post, is housed in an attractive cinder block building with stucco overlay and a metal roof. It sells gas, groceries, and some general merchandise. The original trading post was a small stone building. The present store was built onto the south side of it. Subsequent additions were made across the front around 1940 and at the north end in 1990.

History: Lorenzo Hubbell established the post around 1928. Clarence Wheeler acquired it around 1936, with Harold Springer later becoming a partner, followed by Jay Springer and Gene Wheeler in the early 1970s, John Hickman in 1988, and the current owner, Red Mesa Express, in January, 2000.

West Sun Food Mart
(old Klagetoh Trading Post)

#1 Klagetoh, Ganado, AZ 86505, (928) 674-3387

Located on US 191, 14.5 miles south of Ganado

Description: *Converted.* The store no longer functions as the trading post it was in earlier days. It has been converted into a gas station and small grocery store. The current store is located in a metal building that is an addition built onto the front of the original stone trading post in 1966.

History: Nils Hogner started the post in the 1920s. He took over an existing make-shift store operated out of a small shack by a local Navajo named "Yellow Policeman." Hogner constructed

new buildings and, being an artist, he fixed up the post in an artistic, rustic style using desert plants and rocks placed about the store and house.

Limited information is available about the ownership of the post, but some of the names include Albert Lee in 1936, Lon Wheeler in the 1970s, and Jane Yellowhorse from 1981 to 1990. It was closed for about six months, then Wendell Mortensen acquired it in 1991, Anna Newby in 2004, and the current owner, Red Mesa Express in 2006.

Wide Ruins Trading Post★★

Follow US 191 for 19.8 miles south of Ganado, then turn east onto a dirt road for 3.4 miles to the post. The road goes pass the school and Chapter House and loops back to the highway.

Description: *Abandoned.* Nothing remains of the old post other than the ruins of stone buildings and piles of stone showing where other buildings once stood. The post was originally called **Kinteel Trading Post**. The name comes from the Navajo word "Kinteel," meaning "wide house," which was the name of an Anasazi ruin in the area. Archaeological surveys show that a large prehistoric village once existed in the immediate area of the post.

History: The post was started by Winnie and Spencer Balcomb around 1902. (An earlier post is reported to have been built at the same approximate location by Sam Day around 1895.) Subsequent owners included Wallace Sanders and Peter Parquette (former Navajo Agent), and Bill and Sally Lippincott in 1938, who changed the name from "Kinteel" to "Wide Ruins." The Lippincotts sold it to Carl Hind in 1942 when Bill went into the Navy. They reacquired it after the War in 1945. They sold out to the Navajo tribe in 1950, and it was subsequently operated a few years later by Phil Foutz for the Progressive Mercantile Company, followed by Jim Collyer, Jr. in 1957, Collyer and John Rieffer in 1964, and John and Sharon Rieffer in 1973. It was closed in 1982 following John Rieffer's death. Shortly after, the store and living quarters burned, and the area reverted to ruins again.

Bill and Sally Lippincott worked diligently with the local Navajo weavers to improve the quality of the rugs produced in the area. They are responsible for the renewal of the old-time vegetal-dyed Navajo rugs and a general improvement in the quality of the weaving. Today, vegetal dye rugs from the Wide Ruins area are among the finest Navajo rugs.

OTHER ABANDONED TRADING POSTS

■ **Wildcat:** It was located a short distance north of NM 264, eight miles east of Window Rock. It was started by Gibb Graham about 1940 followed by Jay Smith, A. P. Springstead, and closed about 1962. Nothing remains.

■ **Black Hat:** It was located on the north side of NM 264, six miles east of Window Rock. It was started by Jay Smith in 1948, followed by Eldon Anderson, and Dodd Harris. It closed about 1964. Nothing remains.

■**Divide:** It was located on north side of NM 264, three miles east of Window Rock. It was started by A. Ortega in the early 1900s. Others included Jay Smith and Earl Ashcroft. It closed in 1951. Only ruins remain.

■ **Tse Bonito:** It was located on south side of AZ 264, just west of the New Mexico and Arizona state line. It was started by Lewis Sabin in 1932 and sold in 1957 to Rev. Howard Clark who closed it. Nothing remains.

■ **Rudeau:** It was located in Fort Defiance, Arizona, 1.4 miles west of stoplight, which is 4.4 miles north of Window Rock, AZ on NR 12. It was established by W. E. Hilderbrand around 1915. A. C. Rudeau acquired it in 1938, followed by his son August Rudeau in 1950, Russell Griswold in 1965, August Rudeau again in 1973, and Jane Yellowhorse in 1981. Yellowhorse changed the name to **Fort Defiance Trading Post**. She closed it in 1983, and it sat vacant until it was recently torn down.

■**Dunn Mercantile:** It was located directly across the road from the old Fort Defiance Trading Post. It was started by William Bickel in 1911, followed

Dunn Mercantile Company in the early 1900s. (Museum of New Mexico, #46025)

by William Staggs, Hans Neuman, Lewis Sabin (about 1920), Ray Dunn (1938), O. L. Zimmerman (early 1940s), Vic Walker, Francis Griswold (1950), Willard Palmer (1958), and closed around 1965. It was torn down around 1995, and the site is now a vacant lot. In the 1940s, '50s, and '60s, this was one of the highest volume trading posts on the reservation.

■ **Blacks:** It was located southwest of Fort Defiance — go south .5 mile on NR 112, then east .4 mile to site. The post was established by Anson Damon. Damon's daughter, Nillie, and her husband Alexander Black took it over in 1917, and it became known as **Blacks Trading Post**.

They were followed by Ruth Seal, Black's daughter, in 1954, and her son Walter Seal assumed ownership in 1995. The store is no longer operated as a trading post, although it does open occasionally to sell candy and pop to local children. The original post and adjoining residence are of wood frame construction with a stucco overlay painted light tan. A red sandstone addition was built on the front in 1933, in which the current store is located. The counters, wall shelves, and other furnishings are still present, but no merchandise is carried. The store is now mainly used for storage.

■ **Carson:** It was located on the west side of NR 112, just north of the AZ 264 and NR 112 junction. It was started by Richard Carson prior to 1940 and closed about 1950. Nothing remains.

■ **Karrigan:** It is located on AZ 264 (north side), about one-half mile past AZ 264 and NR 12 intersection, which is 1.8 mi. west of Window Rock. It was established by Joseph Kuhn about 1910, followed by Bob Karrigan about 1940. After Karringan's death his wife ran it, followed by their daughter. The Navajo tribe took it over around 1995 and closed it. The old building is still standing.

■ **Cienega Amarilla:** It is located off NR 12, about eight miles south of Fort Defiance, Arizona. At various times there were a number of trading posts located in the general area known as Cienega Amarillo (Spanish for "yellow marsh"). Some of the traders located there were: Sam Day (about 1888), Caddy Stewart, William Weidemeyer, John Wyant, Joseph Wilkin, William (Billy) Meadows (1895-98), George Manning (1901), and George Sampson (1902). The area was named St. Michaels when a post office was established at the trading post of John Walker and Thomas Osborne in 1902. St. Michaels Mission was established on land owned by Sam Day, and the Mission was first located in the building that Billy Meadows built in 1895 and used briefly as a trading post. The Mission museum is currently housed in this building.

■ **Two Story:** It was located on AZ 264 (north side), 3.2 miles west of Window Rock, Arizona. The building was a large, two-story, wood-frame structure with cement stucco overlay painted light tan. It had the store on the ground floor with living quarters above. The building, which had been greatly vandalized, was burned in 2002. The site has since been cleared. The original post, located directly behind the site where the more recent trading post stood, was started by Charles Day in 1905. In 1915, J. P. Petersen became a partner with Day. Tom Frazier took it over in 1935, built the newer building, and moved the post into it. Lester and Anna Lee bought it in 1941. After Lester's death, Anna Lee continued to operate it. Dick and Betty Harris ran the post for Mrs. Lee from 1970 to 1978. Her son-in-law, Don Barrieault, who ran the post before Harris and again after he left, was shot in a robbery attempt at the store in 1994. Mrs. Lee closed it about a year later.

■ **Hunters Point:** It was located on NR 12 (west side), 6.5 miles south of its junction with AZ 264. All that remains is the shell of a white cinder block building. The post was established by Bob Nicholes around 1940. He was followed by George and Dan Christenson around 1950, Foutz Trading Co. in 1953, and Jack Powell in 1970. Powell closed it in 1989. Another post called **White's Store**,  started around 1916, was located about a mile south and 1/2 mile east of the highway.

■ **Cross Canyon:** It was located on AZ 264, eight miles east of Ganado, Arizona. The original post was started by Charles Manning in the early 1900s. A robbery attempt was made on John Owens, Manning's manager, in 1915. Six years later, another of Manning's managers, Frank Dugan, was killed in a robbery at the post, and the building was burned

down. It was rebuilt several years later at its present location, which is about four miles north of the original site. Other owners included Con Shillingburg in late 1930s, E. T. "Tug" Van in the late 1950s, and John Barr, 1966-85. It was closed in 1987. The store, which was constructed of red sandstone, is still standing, but the interior has been destroyed through salvage of materials and vandalism.

■ **Kinlichee:** It was located about six miles northeast of Ganado. It was established by George Williams in the early 1880s and closed about fifteen years later. Lorenzo Hubbell, Jr. reopened it in 1934 and then closed it in 1938. Nothing remains.

■ **Ganado:** It was located in Ganado just north of the AZ 264/US 191 junction. It was established by Bickel & Co. in 1928. Albert Lee took it over in 1929 and later turned it over to his son Hugh Lee, who was followed by J. B. Tanner in 1954. Art Lee, Hugh's brother, acquired it in 1956 with his son-in-law, Joe Danoff, as manager. Danoff became the owner in 1967. Gordon Gorman bought it in 1981, and it was destroyed by fire that same year. Gorman did not reopen the trading post but operates a cafe in the old residence next door.

■ **Round Top:** It was located .7 mile east of Ganado and .5 mile north of AZ 264. It was started by Herbert Shillingburg in the early 1930s,

followed by Clarence Wheeler, Clyde Theise in 1949, and Gordon Gorman in 1976. Gorman closed it in 1997. The post no longer operates, but the building is in good condition and the adjoining residence is currently occupied by the last owner.

■ **Cornfields:** It was located off NR 15A, 1.2 miles east of NR 15 and eight miles south of AZ 264. The post was established by Lorenzo Hubbell around 1896 and operated by Sam Day, Ed Thatcher, Jim Karigan, and Charles Cousins, among others. It is reported to have closed around 1928. Nothing remains.

■ **Burntwater:** It was located about five miles north of US I-40. Leave the highway at exit 343 (two miles east of Sanders, Arizona) and follow the road north and east, turn left onto NR 9010 for three miles to the

fork, then go left for .7 mile to the last trading post location. The post was relocated on the main road in a metal Quonset hut which is still present. The original post is about 300 yards west across the wash. The stone ruins of the original post remain.

It was a fairly large post, and most of the stone walls are still present, but the roof has fallen in. The post was established by Burris N. Barnes in the early 1900s. Stanley Smith took it over in 1930 and moved the trading post into the Quonset hut. Other owners included Don Jacobs, Sr. in 1967, and E. Brady Smithson from 1974 until 1983, when it closed. The original post got its name when a shade ramada caught fire and burning parts fell into the water. It was known by the local Navajos as Burntwater from then on.

■ **Pine Springs:** It was located about 11.5 miles north of US I-40. Leave the highway at exit 343 and follow NR 9010 toward Burntwater.

Keep right at the fork and go 9.7 miles to the site. The old post was well-constructed of red sandstone. The walls are still standing, but the interior was destroyed by fire in 1975, a few years after it closed. The post's

origin is uncertain, but it is believed that Curt Cronemeyer may have started it in the 1880s. Other early owners were George McAdams and C. D. Richardson. Bill Stahle bought it in the early 1930s and sold it to Homer Boyd, followed by Bill Lippincott around 1939. Lippincott turned it over to the Navajo tribe in the early 1940s, and it was operated for them by Jim Ashcroft. Dan Christenson took it over in 1955, followed by Ira Hatch in 1956, Russell Griswold in 1964, and Norman Ashcroft in 1967 until he closed it in 1971.

■ **Rocky Point:** It was located twelve miles west of Gallup, NM, on old Hwy. 66. It was started by Al Tietjen in the 1930's. It was abandoned when Interstate 40 was built over the site.

■ **Sanders:** It was located on the Rio Puerco of the West in the vicinity of Sanders, Arizona. It was established by George Sampson in 1883. Joseph Schmedding is reported to have been there in 1918. Others included Spencer Balcomb and A. C. Coon. When it closed is unknown.

■ **Cedar Point:** It was located two miles east of Sanders. It was started by H. W. Gibson in the late 1930s. C. G. Wallace and John Kennedy bought it in 1945. Robert Jones operated the store from 1947 until it was abandonded when Interstate 40 was built over the site for the Cedar Point Interchange.

■ **Houck:** The post's approximate location was off US I-40 about thirty-two miles west of Gallup. It was established by James D. Houck in 1874 and sold in 1885. Various traders ran it until 1910, when George McAdams bought it and sold it in 1919. It closed for good around 1922. Houck was one of the earliest trading posts outside the Fort Defiance area. The actual site was not located, but it is doubtful if anything remains, since it ceased operating over eighty years ago. Billy Burke owned a post about five miles from Houck, and another one called **White Mound** (where Fort Courage is currently located) was started by Joe Grubbs —both were started around 1920. A post was started at Allentown, a few miles east of Houck, in the early 1880s by Curt Cronemeyer, who (along with his clerk Charles Brewer) were killed in 1915 in a robbery at the post.

■ **Lupton:** It was located along old US 66 about twenty-four miles west of Gallup. It was owned by Al Frick in the 1940s and closed in 1963. There were several other trading posts in the Lupton area, all of which no longer exist. They included **Three Hogans** started in the 1920s by Jack Hill and sold to Vic Walker, followed by Jim Ashcroft in 1949-52, Richard Sellers in the 1960s, and closed in the early 1990s. **Box Canyon** was owned by LeRoy Atchinson in the late 30s. **Lookout** was owned by Dan Hunter. **Stateline** was owned by J. W. Bennett in the 1940s.

■ **Manuelito:** It was located north of US I-40, about thirteen miles west of Gallup. It was started by Hyde Exploring Expedition around 1878; Lorenzo Hubbell owned it in 1884; Stephen Aldrich and James Bennett acquired it in 1885; Bennett sold out the same year to Elias Clark, who then sold his share to Archibald Sweetland in 1886; Aldrich was still an owner in 1903; Mike Kirk owned it in 1920 and sold it to A. P Gonzales in 1945. It closed shortly after 1963. Nothing remains.

Chapter 7

Keams Canyon

L&A Trading Post, Keams Canyon, Hopi Res. '96

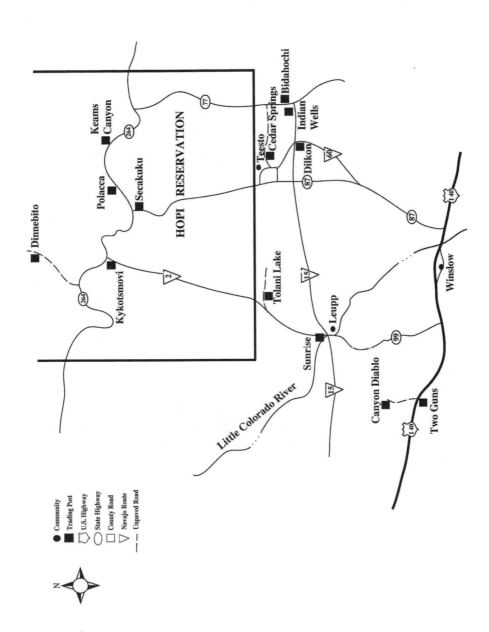

Keams Canyon Trading Post★★★

Keams Canyon Shopping Center, P. O. Box 607, Keams Canyon, AZ 86034, (928) 738-2295

Located on AZ 264, 81 miles east of its junction with US 160 at Tuba City or 45 miles west of Ganado.

Description: *Converted.* The current store is located in a large, cream colored building, which has a grocery store on one end, a restaurant on the other, and an art gallery in the middle. There is also a motel and gas station. Keam's old trading post is incorporated within the existing building, which has been greatly enlarged and modernized by Bill and Cliff McGee. The art gallery includes an outstanding Indian arts and crafts store with a large selection of Hopi kachina dolls and baskets, Navajo rugs, jewelry, and paintings. A unique red-black-gray-white rug is produced by weavers from the Keams Canyon-Pinon areas. Although very similiar to the Ganado, it is distinctive in both design and size. The design features big bold patterns, and it is usually much larger in size, one being as large as 14 x 26 feet.

Keams Canyon Shopping Center, located on the site of Thomas Keam's second trading post, 2000.

History: The original trading post was named after Thomas Keam who, with his brother William, came to the post in 1875 (he actually bought out a trader, who had been there a few years earlier). Keam was born in Cornwall, England in 1846 and came to this country around 1861. In 1865, he enlisted with the First New Mexico Volunteer Cavalry and served for a year and a half. While serving with the cavalry, he made his first visit to the canyon that now bears his name. It had been known as Peach Orchard Springs. While in the army he learned to speak both Navajo and Hopi. After his discharge, he worked as an interpreter at Fort Defiance, and later was appointed special agent for the Navajos. He was never able to obtain the position he desperately desired, that of Navajo Indian Agent, due to a conflict with Pueblo Indian Agent W. F. M. Arny, whom he considered hypocritical and unfair in his dealings with the Indians. Arny made slanderous accusations about Keam to officials in Washington.

The site chosen for his trading post was about two miles below the head of the canyon under the eave of the canyon's north wall. The original post was a small stone building and corral. After six years the post had

Overlooking the early Keams Canyon Trading Post at the original site, about 1885. (Museum of New Mexico, #16473)

The second Keams Canyon Trading Post was located at the mouth of the canyon, 1906. (Courtesy of The Museum of Northen Arizona, Photo Archives #MS 168-6-25)

grown to about a dozen buildings consisting of his four-room residence, the trading post building, wareroom, blacksmith and carpenter shops, stables and wagon sheds, and small employee and guest buildings. All buildings were constructed of dressed stone with timber and board roofs overlaid with clay.

In 1886, Keam offered to rent part of his trading post building to the Secretary of Interior for use as an Indian Industrial School. His initial offer was not accepted. In 1887, he offered to rent all his facilities for $100 per month. This offer was accepted, and he moved about a half-mile below the mouth of the canyon (where Keams Canyon Shopping Center now stands) and built a new home and trading post. Two years later, after additional negotiations, he sold all his original property to the government for use as a BIA boarding school for $10,000, less than half his asking price. In 1902, he sold his new trading post to his friend Lorenzo Hubbell, who bought it for his son, Lorenzo, Jr., to run. He then returned to England for a visit. While there he suffered a heart attack and died about a year later.

Subsequent owners of the post after Hubbell included Joseph Schmedding (1918), E. P. Halderman (1924), Bill McGee with partners Clarence Wheeler and Harold Springer (1938), Bill and Cliff McGee (1941), McGee and Sons (Cliff, Farron and Bruce McGee, and Johnny Kay) (1970), and Ron McGee and Johnny Kay, 2003 to present.

Polacca Trading Post

P. O. Box 188, Keams Canyon, AZ 86034, (928) 737-2677

Located on AZ 264, 11 miles west of Keams Canyon.

Description: *Converted.* The store, currently called Polacca Circle M, is housed in a somewhat plain, cream colored cinder block building with the roof extending out over the front. It operates as a small, self-service grocery store and no longer functions as a trading post.

The earlier Polacca Trading Post, about 1940s. It burned in 1969. (Photo courtesy of Grace Herring)

History: The original post in the area was reported to have been established by Lorenzo Hubbell in 1891. Tom Pavatea, a Hopi, started a post in 1943 located about .3 mile east of the current store at the junction of the highway and the road that goes up to First Mesa (possibly the same site as Hubbell's post). Pavatea's post was made of stone and later had cinder block additions. It was sold to Bill and Cliff McGee in 1950, and it burned in 1969. The current store was built by Paul and Rose Humphrey right after the old one burned and has been leased to the McGees ever since.

Secakuku Trading Post

P. O. Box 668, Second Mesa, AZ 86043, (928) 737-2632

Located at the junction of AZ 264 and AZ 87, 18 miles west of Keams Canyon.

Description: *Closed.* The store closed in early 2005 but hopefully will reopen in the near future. It is housed in a large, attractive building with stucco overlay painted light tan, and vegas extending out the front. The interior is a large self-service grocery store.

History: The original trading post is still in good condition and used as a residence. It is located near the top of Second Mesa at the village of Sipaulovi. The post was started by Hale Secakuku in 1933. In 1960, he and his son Ferrell built a second store down by the highway. Hale Secakuku's wife continued to operate the original store until shortly after Hale's death in 1974. The second store sold groceries and general merchandise, but no longer functioned as a trading post. It currently houses the post office and a small cafe. Ferrell Secakuku built the current store in 1982 and his daughter Bonnie Secakuku, is the current owner.

Kykotsmovi Village Store*

P. O. Box 655 Kykotsmovi, AZ 86039, (928) 734-2456

Located at the village of Kykotsmovi (formerly New Oraibi), which is about 23 miles west of Keams Canyon and .5 mile south of Highway AZ 264.

Description: *Converted:* The store is in an attractive building made of rough-faced cement blocks painted light tan with a rustic entrance enhanced by log posts. It is built onto the original trading post, which is still in use as a warehouse. The store sells groceries and general merchandise but no longer functions as a trading post.

History: The post was reported to have been started by F. W. Volz around 1897. It was known as the **Oraibi Trading Post** when Lorenzo

Hubbell bought it in 1905. His son Lorenzo Hubbell, Jr. took it over from 1920 until 1951, when Babbitt Bros. acquired it. J. H. McAdams is reported to have owned a trading post for a short time at New Oraibi, which may have been the same store. The date is unknown, but it was probably in the late 1880s before Volz. In 1996, the Kykotsmovi Village acquired the store and are the present owners. Tommy and Julie Canyon are the managers.

Dinnebito Trading Post★★
P. O. Box 109, Hotevilla, AZ 86030, (928) 527-2037

> *Located on NR 62, 8.4 miles north of AZ 264; junction is just west of Dinnebito Wash and about 15 miles west of the Hopi Cultural Center.*

Description: *Closed.* The store was housed in an attractive building of cement block construction painted a light cream color with a metal

roof and a large attached warehouse of the same construction. There is also an adjacent stone building and a large metal storage building. Out back is a corral and a cement block

residence. The interior of the store which was recently closed was last a typical small self-service grocery store with some general merchandise and video rentals.

History: An earlier trading post was located on Dinnebito Wash about twenty miles south of the current store. It was started by Lorenzo Hubbell in 1911, followed by his son Lorenzo Hubbell, Jr. Another store was started in 1955 by J. C. Harrison with Rosco McGee as a partner. In 1958, Vernon Bloomfield acquired the store, and the following year it burned down. Bloomfield rebuilt the store and sold it to Elijah Blair in 1960. Blair remodeled and enlarged the store, then closed it in 1991. It sat vacant until 1993 when Harry Yazzie reopened it and renamed it **Rocky Ridge General Store**. It was again closed around the end of 2006.

Bitahochee Trading Post★★

Located about 100 yards east of AZ 77, .3 mile north of its junction with NR 15.

Description: *Abandoned.* This was a picturesque old post. All the buildings still standing are in fair condition, but the interiors have been destroyed. The main structure is a combination of several buildings joined together and is made of various materials (cut stone, cinder blocks, and wood). The main part of the building, where the store was located, was made of wood frame  construction with a stucco overlay painted red. It was built onto the old stone trading post, which was originally built for a stage coach station in the 1870s and had small openings built into the walls for gun ports.

History: The post was established by Julius Wetzler in 1880. Information about subsequent owners is unknown until Jot Stiles acquired it in the late-1930s and then sold it to Ray Hunt around 1942. Bill McGee and Harry Folk acquired it in 1945, and Bill's brother, Cliff, joined the partnership in 1955. In 1962, the McGees sold out to Folk, who then sold it to Herb Huckradie. Subsequent owners included Hans Nielson and Lark Washburn in 1964, Lark Washburn and Sam Christensen in

Bitahochee Trading Post, 1949. (Museum of New Mexico, #46037)

1970, Sam Christensen in 1978, and Phil Foutz and his son Brian from 1988 until 1989. The Navajo tribe took it over and closed it for good in 1994.

The grave of a US Cavalry soldier who was stationed in the area in the late 1870s is located on the hillside about thirty-five yards directly behind the main building. There is a white stone marker that appears to be of fairly recent origin with the inscription: "Theo. Thysing" "Co. C" "4 U. S. Cav."

Indian Wells Trading Post
P. O. Box 3158, Indian Wells. AZ 89031, (928) 654-3390

Located about .5 mile west of AZ 77; turnoff is .3 mile north of the AZ 77/NR 15 junction. (Directly across highway from Bidahochi TP.)

Description: *Converted.* The current Indian Wells store is housed in a rectangular metal building painted white with the roof extending out over the front, forming an awning. It is operated as a modern gas and grocery convenience store.

History: The original Indian Wells Trading Post was located about a half mile behind the current store, just beyond a large, black gravel quarry operation. It was housed in a large stone building. J. H. McAdams owned it in 1909, followed by Hubert Richardson in 1910, Slim Halderman in 1924. It was sold to Babbitt Bros. in the late 1930s. They closed it around 1975, and it burned in 1979. Nothing remains except some stone rubble.

Old Indian Wells Trading Post, 1958. (Courtesy of Museum of Northern Arizona, Photo Archives #74.672)

The more recent Indian Wells store is actually a successor to the **Bitahochee Trading Post**. In 1989, Phil Foutz and his son Brian lost the lease on Bitahochee, and Brian moved a short distance north and started a store in a trailer on church-leased land. He was made to move because commercial use would have cost the church its tax-exemption. Phil moved the store to the present Indian Wells location around 1990, then sold out to Thriftway Corp. in 1996, which subsequently transferred it to Red Mesa Express, the present owner.

Dilkon Trading Post

Located approximately .2 mile south of NR 15 at Dilkon,
which is six miles east of the NR 15/AZ 87 junction.

Description: *Closed.* The owner has plans to remodel the store and open it full-time. It was operated as a small convenience store and no longer functions as a trading post. It was originally constructed of native stone and subsequently covered with stucco overlay and painted light tan. It is an attractive building with more of the old trading post appearance, as opposed to more modern convenience stores.

History: The trading post was established by J. W. Bush in 1919. Lorenzo Hubbell, Jr. owned it in 1935-36. Later owners included Harold Springer and Francis Powell in 1968, Jay Springer in 1973, and the present owners, Dan Roberts and Darlene Begay, in 1992.

Cedar Springs Trading Post★★

Located about 5.1 miles north of Dilcon on NR 60 and
then .8 mile east of NR 601.

Description: *Abandoned.* The post apparently was well built since the walls are still standing and are in relatively good condition. It was made of chiseled native stone with adobe mortar. The interior walls were

covered with an adobe stucco overlay. It was a three room post, possibly with the store in the center and the wareroom on one end and living quarters on the other.

Another stone building was located across the road from the front of the store. Behind the post (across the existing road) twin hogans still stand, probably built for visiting Navajo customers to stay in while they carried out their trading.

History: The post was started by Jake Tobin in 1885. Lorenzo Hubbell acquired it in 1909. It was operated by his younger brother, Charles Hubbell, from 1909 until 1911 and again from 1918 until 1919. That year Charles was killed at the post in a robbery and the post burned down. It was rebuilt and then closed for good around 1940.

Sunrise Trading Post★★

Located approximately .8 mile east of the current Leupp store, about equal distance between two old bridges — one over the Little Colorado river and the other over Canyon Diablo.

Description: *Abandoned.* The original trading post was housed in a large stone building. It has stucco overlay, painted white, which may have been applied in more recent years. The building is still standing, but it is in poor condition.

History: The trading post was built by Babbitt's employee, H.W. "Nebby" Smith, in 1920. The Babbitts owned another trading post in the area around Tolchaco. Business was poor there, and Smith, without the Babbitts' knowledge or consent, began building a large stone building to replace the Tolchaco post. After finally getting approval, the building was completed and became the Sunrise Trading Post. Smith subsequently became a partner. C. D. Richardson acquired the post in 1928 and sold it to Stanton K Borum in 1935. Borum then sold out to Elmer McGee in 1937. Subsequent owners included Harold Springer and Francis Powell in 1950, and Jay Springer in 1973, following his father's death. Springer closed it in 1985.

Tolani Lake Trading Post
HC-61 PMB 3000, Winslow, AZ 86047, (928) 686-6296

Located approximately 9.6 miles north of Leupp on NR 2, then four miles east on NR 24.

Description: *Closed.* The store was housed in a plain cinder block building painted white. It operated as a small self-service grocery store and no longer functioned as a trading post. Nothing remains of the original post which was located about 100 yards east of the present store.

History: The original trading post, known as **Red Lake Trading Post**, was reported to have been started around 1891. Some of the early owners were Billy Williams, followed by the Richardsons and partner Stanton Borum with Billy Young as the operator until 1942. It was run as a co-op store from 1945 until it burned down in 1953. It was reported to have been operated at a couple different locations close by until Bill

Montgomery acquired it around 1960 and set up a store at a temporary location while he constructed the current building. After he left in 1968 the store was closed until Dina Coldren and Stanley Tsosie acquired it in 1996. They were followed in 1998 by Ervin and Laverne Tso, who closed it in 2000.

Canyon Diablo Trading Post★★★

From I-40 Exit 230, which is 22 miles west of Winslow, go north 3.6 miles to railroad tracks; cross the tracks and go .3 mile to the site.

Description:*Abandoned.* The stone walls of an exceptionally large building (over 200 feet long and 40 feet wide) are still standing. All other buildings that once occupied the site no longer exist.

History: In 1882, the Atlantic & Pacific Railroad was just being built through the area, and it was necessary to construct a high iron bridge,

Old Canyon Diablo railroad bridge, 1883. (Museum of New Mexico #15514)

over 500 feet long and 250 feet high, across Canyon Diablo. A small temporary town of railroad workers was established on the east side of the canyon. It soon became a hangout for outlaws and was known as one of the toughest towns in the Southwest with almost daily killings. There were gambling houses, saloons, and bordellos in temporary tarpaper, wood, and tin shacks strung out along the north side of the railroad tracks. Shortly after the community started, Charles Algert opened a small store in an abandoned boxcar. When work on the bridge was completed and the railroad workers moved on, the town faded away. Algert converted his store into a trading post for the Indians. He later built a huge stone trading post, the ruins of which are still present, and sold it to Frederick Volz in 1897. Volz remained in business there for the next fifteen years before selling out to Babbitt Bros. in 1912. The Babbitts either sold or closed the old stone trading post in 1922. They moved south to old Highway 66, where they opened a new store that later burned down in 1934. Lorenzo Hubbell, Jr. operated the trading post at Canyon Diablo from 1929 until 1932, probably out of the same stone building. Jot Stiles is reported to have owned it from around 1938 until 1942 or '43, which may be the year it finally closed.

Two Guns Trading Post★★

Located on the south side of I-40 at Exit 230, which is 22 miles west of Winslow.

Description: *Closed.* Some might call Two Guns Trading Post, until it closed a few years ago, just another tourist stop along I-40; but, this former Route 66 tourist attraction had much more potential than that. During its heyday in the 1940s, '50s, and '60s, when old Route 66 passed by its front door, there existed a wild animal zoo, the Apache Death Cave where tours were conducted, the original concrete bridge where Route 66 crossed Canyon Diablo (which is listed in the National Register of Historic Places), and numerous old stone buildings, all of which could be restored. The most recent facilities were a combination service station, gift shop, mini-mart, and a KOA campground. The business was closed around 1998, but there are rumors of plans to reopen and restore the original Two Guns site.

History: There have been trading posts or stores in the vicinity of Two Guns since pioneer days, but little is known about their origin. The name "Two Guns" was first given to the area when Earl Cundiff acquired the property in 1923. Shortly after Cundiff built his first stone trading post, Highway 66 (then known as the Old Trails Highway) was rerouted and passed by his store. In 1925, Harry "Indian" Miller, an Apache, leased the store from Cundiff. While there he started the wild animal zoo and developed the Apache Death Cave as tourist attractions. The cave was reported to have been the site where a number of Apaches took refuge after they raided a Navajo camp and stole several horses. The Navajos gave chase and the Apaches hid in the cave and died of suffocation when the Navajos built fires at the entrance. Miller nearly lost his life near the cave when he was attacked by a mountain lion. He is said to have shot and killed Cundiff in 1926 in what was judged to be self-defense. The interior of the store burned later the same year. Miller left in 1930, and the store was leased to several people, including Earl Tinnan of Flagstaff (1933-35) and Phillip Hesch. When Highway 66 was again rerouted around 1938, Hesch moved the store to a location on the new highway a short distance north of the old bridge. S. I. Richardson owned it from 1957 until his death in 1959, with Toney Richardson acting as manager from 1958 until 1961 when the post was sold to Two Guns, Inc.. In 1971, an explosion and fire destroyed the trading post, cafe, motel, and service station, and it was subsequently rebuilt at its present location. In 1992, the 320-acre site was bought by Howard Armstrong, who, with the aid of old photos, documents, and personal interviews, plans to restore Two Guns to its former historic heyday.

OTHER ABANDONED TRADING POSTS

■ **Jeddito:** It was also known as **Antelope Springs**. It was located 4.5 miles west of Keams Canyon and 1.4 miles north of AZ 264. The site is .2 mile north of the Chapter House. It was established in 1906. Owners included J. H. McAdams, Babbitt Bros., Kenneth Adair, Lester Lee, and Charles Gallagher, who closed it around 1972. Nothing remains.

■ **L & A:** It was located just off AZ 264 at the Hopi Indian Agency, south of the post office. It was started by Skeet Stiles around 1930, and was later owned by Lester Lee in 1948, and Jack Lee in 1954 who closed it in 1975. The original building, made of red sandstone, is still in good condition. The building is currently used by a local church.

■ **Conley, Favella,** and **Sharp:** They were located in Keams Canyon area and owned by Babbitt Bros. in the late 1890s. No other information is available and their sites were not located.

■ **Coal Mine Mesa:** It was located on AZ 264, twenty-four miles west of Tuba City, Arizona. Little information is available about the early ownership. Vernon Young sold it to Bill and Cliff McGee in 1962, and they closed it in 1968. A cinder block building in poor condition remains.

■ **Sand Springs:** It was located thirteen miles south of Old Oraibi on NR 2, then eighteen miles west on NR 58. Lorenzo Hubbell, Jr. started the post around 1922 and closed it in 1945. Nothing remains.

■ **White Cone:** It was located .1 mile east of AZ 77, 9.8 miles south of the AZ 264 and AZ 77 junction. It was started by Fancy Nelson in 1916, followed by Albert Lee (1930), Clarence Wheeler and Harold Springer (1935) with Francis Powell becoming the operator in 1943. Jay Springer became a partner after his father's death in 1973, and Gene Wheeler became a partner a short time later after his father died. They closed the post in 1985. All that remains is a cement slab and an old, wooden residence.

■ **Na-Ah-Tee:** It was located on NR 9065, 3.4 miles west of AZ 77, and 18.5 miles south of AZ 264. The post is reported to have been started around 1900, by a party unknown. Lorenzo Hubbell, Jr. owned it in 1933 and sold it to Kyle Bales in 1951. Other owners included the partnership of C. E. Wheeler, J. B. Tanner, and Bill and Cliff McGee in 1954; Bill McGee and Charles McGee in 1955; Charles McGee in 1959; and Harold Springer and Francis Powell in 1965. The lease

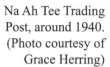

Na Ah Tee Trading
Post, around 1940.
(Photo courtesy of
Grace Herring)

reverted to the Navajo tribe in 1970, and they closed it around 1973. The White Cone Chapter ran it for a couple years as a co-op, then closed it. It burned in 1976. Only the chimney and stone rubble remain.

■ **Teesto:** It was located .2 mile north of NR 60. The turnoff is 1.4 miles east of AZ 87, just before the Teesto Chapter House. It was started by Jimmy McJunkin around 1915. McJunkin died in 1970. His wife and son continued to run it with assistance from various managers until around 1981 when it closed. Only stone rubble remains.

■ **Castle Butte:** It was located about 1 mile west of NR 60. The turnoff is 6.1 miles south of the NR 60 and NR 15 junction at Dilkon. It was started in 1906 by a party unknown. It was abandoned for several years when Jot Stiles acquired it in 1934. He sold it to Ross Vernon in 1955. The date of closure is unknown. Part of the walls and other stone rubble are all that remain.

■ **Old Leupp:** It was located about two miles east of Leupp on NR 15, then two miles south on NR 6932. Nothing remains of the trading post except a chimney and a pile of stone rubble. The post was established by John Walker around 1910. Hubert Richardson bought it in 1914. Stanton K. Borum became a partner around 1920 and later bought it in 1928. Following Borum's death in 1935, his wife continued to operate the post until 1944, when she sold it to Elmer McGee. Ralph McGee, Elmer's son, later became the owner in 1967 and closed it in 1980. The community of Leupp was named for Francis Leupp, Indian Commissioner. During World War II a prisoner of war camp was located nearby.

■ **Tolchaco:** Turn off NR 15 about .9 mile west of Leupp store onto NR 6910, a dirt, single-track road. Go 6.5 miles and turn right .7 mile to the site, which is located in a grove of old, scattered cottonwood trees. Stone ruins are all that remain, but it is an interesting area to visit. The post was started by John Walker in 1905 and sold in 1910. There were several traders after Walker, including David Ward, who worked for Walker. Babbitt Bros. bought it in 1918 and closed it in the early 1920s shortly after a bridge was built across Canyon Diablo close to old Leupp. This spelled the end for the trading post.

■ **Wolf:** Follow the directions to Tolchaco, except at the turnoff 6.5 miles in go straight ahead. After about a mile there will be two gates about 1/2 mile apart. Turn right just after the second gate and go .1 mile to site. The ruins of the stone walls are still standing. The post was established by Herman Wolf in 1868 and was the first one on the Little Colorado River. After Wolf's death in 1899, George McAdams and his nephew S. I. Richardson acquired it. In 1901, Babbitt Bros. became a partner, and it was sold shortly after to Leander Smith in 1902. Smith was forced to close the post in 1904 as the result of a practical joke in which he placed a human skull in the front window. Because of the Navajo belief in the chindi (death spirit) they would not enter the store.

■ **Benton Mesa:** The site was not located. Its approximate location is on the Little Colorado River a few miles upriver from Wolf Trading Post. It was established by George McAdams in 1902, sold to R. M. Bruchman in 1904, and closed shortly after.

■ **Steckel:** The site was not located. The general location is at Sandwater in the Tolchaco area. It was started by Carl Steckel in 1920 in partnership with Babbitt Bros. and closed a few years later.

■ **Black Falls:** The site was not located. Its approximate location is just north of Black Falls on the west side of the Little Colorado River. The original post was built by Samuel Preston in 1888, followed by Fred Volz, 1891-1893. Emmet Kellam operated a post in the area in the late 1930s. He sold it to B. B. Bonner in 1952. After a couple other owners it finally closed in 1964. Across the river in the same vicinity Jack and Glen Taylor ran a post in an old wooden building from 1935 until 1941.

BIBLIOGRAPHY

BOOKS

Babbitt, James E., Martha Blue, Willow Roberts, and Jean Brundige-Baker. *Historic Trading Posts*. Flagstaff, Museum of Northern Arizona Press, 1991.

Blue, Martha. *Indian Trader, Life and Times of J. L. Hubbell*. Walnut, CA, Kiva Publishing, 2000.

Clark, H. Jackson. *The Owl in the Monument: And Other Stories from Indian Country*. Salt Lake City , University of Utah Press, 1993.

Counselor, Jim, and Ann Counselor. *Wild, Woolly, and Wonderful*. New York, Vantage Press, 1954.

Cousins, Jean, and Bill Cousins. *Tales from Wide Ruins*. Lubbock, Texas Tech University Press, 1994.

Dollar, Tom. *Indian Country: A Guide to Northeastern Arizona*. Tucson, Arizona Highways, 1993.

Eddington, Patrick, and Susan Makov. *Trading Post Guidebook: Where to Find the Trading Post, Galleries, Auctions, Artists, and Museums of the Four Corners Region*. Flagstaff, Northland Publishing, 1995.

Forrest, Earle R. *With a Camera in Old Navajoland*. Norman, University of Oklahoma Press, 1969

Faunce, Hilda. *Desert Wife*. Lincoln, University of Nebraska Press, 1961.

Gibson , Walter. Nakai Toh: *My Days with the Finest People on God's Green Earth*. Bountiful, Utah, Family History Publishers, 1994.

Gillmor, Frances, and Louisa Wade Wetherill. *Traders to the Navajos: The Story of theWetherills of Kayenta*. Albuquerque, University of New Mexico Press, 1953.

Gilpin, Laura. *The Enduring Navajo*. Austin, University of Texas Press, 1968.

Graves, Laura. *Thomas Barke Keam, Indian Trader*. Norman, University of Oklahoma Press, 1998.

Hall, Edward T. *West of the Thirties: Discoveries Among the Navajo and Hopi.* New York, Doubleday Publishing, 1994.

Hegemann, Elizabeth Compton. *Navajo Trading Days.* Albuquerque, University of New Mexico Press, 1963.

Houk, Rose. *Navajo of Canyon de Chelly.* Tucson, Southwest Parks and Monuments Association, 1995.

James, H. L. *Rugs and Posts.* West Chester, PA, Schiffer Publishing, Ltd., 1988.

Kennedy, Mary Jeanette. *Tales of a Trader's Wife.* Albuquerque, Valiant, 1965.

Klinck, Richard E. *Land of Room Enough and Time Enough.* Albuquerque, University of New Mexico Press, 1953.

Kosik, Fran. *Native Roads: A Complete Motoring Guide to the Navajo and Hopi Nations.* Flagstaff, Creative Solutions Publishing, 1996.

Lee, Albert Hugh, and Ella Ruth Lee Danoff. *Gaamaliitsoh Indian Trader: An Autobiography of Albert Hugh Lee (1897-1976).* Mesa, AZ, Lofgreen's, Inc., 1982.

Linford, Laurance D. *Navajo Places: History, Legend, Landscape.* Salt Lake City, University of Utah Press, 2000.

Locke, Raymond Friday. *The Book of the Navajo.* Los Angeles, Mankind Publishing Co., 1976.

MacDonald, Eleanor D., and John B. Arrington. *The San Juan Basin: My Kingdom Was a County.* Denver, MIDO Printing Co., 1970.

Maxwell, Gilbert S. *Navajo Rugs: Past, Present & Future.* Santa Fe, Southwest Images, 1992.

McNitt, Frank. *Richard Wetherill: Anasazi.* Albuquerque, University of New Mexico Press, 1957.

McNitt, Frank. *The Indian Traders.* Oklahoma City, University of Oklahoma Press, 1962.

Mercurio, Gian, and Maxymilian L. Peschel. *The Guide to Trading Post and Pueblos.* Cortez, CO, Lonewolf Publishing, 1994.

Richardson, Gladwell. *Navajo Trader.* Tucson, University of Arizona Press, 1991.

Richardson, Gladwell. *Two Guns Arizona.* Santa Fe, Blue Feathers Press, 1968.

Roberts, Willow. *Stokes Carson: Twentieth Century Trading on the Navajo Reservation.* Albuquerque, University of New Mexico Press, 1987.

Rodee, Marian E. *Old Navajo Rugs: Their Development from 1900 to 1940.* Albuquerque, University of New Mexico Press, 1981.

Schmedding, Joseph. *Cowboy and Indian Trader.* Caldwell, ID, The Caxton Printing, 1951.

Underhill, Ruth. *The Ñavajos.* Norman, University of Oklahoma Press, 1956.

Woods, Susan E. and Robert S. McPherson. *Along Navajo Trails.* Logan, Utah State University Press, 2005.

ARTICLES

Abbott, C. and Ester Henderson "Along the Trading Post Trail." *Arizona Highways,* June, 1943.

Brenner, Malcolm. "Is the Four Corners Ready for Cafe Teec?" *Farmington Daily Times,* April, 1996.

Brown, Jo. "Indian Traders of North America." *Arizona Highways,* May, 1973.

Cohen, Steve. "Hubbell Trading Post." *Cross Currents,* August, 1997.

DeLauer, Marjel. "A Century of Indian Traders and Trading Posts." *Arizona Highways,* March, 1975.

Douglas, Thomas. "The West Comes Alive! Two Guns Arizona." *Trading Post News,* February, 1996.

Guterson, Ben. "The Vanishing Trading Post." *New Mexico Magazine,* August, 1994.

Guterson, Ben. "Trading Post Preserves Spirit of Times Past." *The (Gallup) Independent,* February, 1992.

Guterson, Ben. "Wetherill Murder: Lots of Mysteries Here." *Native Sun Newspaper,* July, 1991

Jacka, Lois Essary. "The Legend of Hubbell Trading Post." *Arizona Highways,* January, 1997.

Jeffers, Jo. "Hubbell Trading Post National Historic Site." *Arizona Highways,* September, 1967.

Lowe, Sam. "The Little World of Black Mountain." *Arizona Highways,* August, 1979.

Manchester, Ann, and Albert Manchester. "Treasure House of the Southwest." *Highways (the Good Sam Club Magazine)*, August, 1997.

McCoy, Ron. Naalye'he'Ba'hooghan: Where Past Is Present." *Arizona Highways*, June, 1987.

Pyle, Frank. "The Uprising of Polk and Posey in 1915." March, 1991.

Richardson, Toney. "Traders at Tonalea." *Desert Magazine*, January, 1948.

Richardson, Gladwell. "Bonanza in the Ghost Post." *Desert Magazine*, July, 1966.

Taylor, Paul. "Two Guns Arizona." *Route 66 Magazine*, Winter, 1993/94.

Thomas, Bob. "The Phantom of Willow Springs." *Arizona Highways*, January, 1997.

VanValkenburgh, Richard, and John C. McPhee. "A Short History of the Navajo People." Window Rock, U. S. Dept. of Interior, Navajo Service, 1938.

VanValkenburgh, Richard. ''Henry Chee Dodge Chief of the Navajo Nation." *Arizona Highways*, July, 1943.

Ward, Susan Bayer. "Mike Goulding's Treasure House in Monument Valley." *Arizona Highways*, September, 1991.

Winslowe, John R. "Navajo Traders for Many Moons." *True West*, April, 1969.

INDEX of TRADING POSTS

ABOUT THE AUTHOR

The author, a native of Missouri, is retired after 34 years in the forestry profession. He currently lives in Durango, Colorado with his wife, Judy. His interest in western history and appreciation of the high desert southwest, combined with the fact that many of the old trading posts are rapidly disappearing, led him to write this book. He has traveled extensively throughout the Four Corners region visiting and researching the numerous sites.